D1766211

DISJECTA

Miscellaneous Writings and a
Dramatic Fragment
by
Samuel Beckett
Edited with a foreword by Ruby Cohn

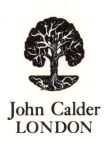

John Calder
LONDON

This book first published 1983 in Great Britain by
John Calder (Publishers) Ltd.,
18, Brewer Street,
London W1R 4AS

British Library Cataloguing in Publication Data
Beckett, Samuel
  Disjecta
  I. title   II. Cohn, Ruby
  824'.914   PR6003. E282

ISBN 0 7145 3974 0 casebound
ISBN 0 7145 4016 1 paperback

SUBSIDISED BY THE
Arts Council
OF GREAT BRITAIN

Typeset in 10 on 12 point Janson by Alan Sutton Publishing Ltd., Gloucester.

Printed by Photobooks (Bristol) Ltd, Bristol
Bound by Robert Hartnoll Ltd, Bodmin

CONTENTS

Foreword

Disjecta is Beckett's own title for this miscellany of criticism and a dramatic fragment. Unpublished or published obscurely, these pieces have been available only in a few fortunate libraries. It is in generosity to scholars — on the special plea of Dr James Acheson — that Samuel Beckett now permits the publication of material which he belittles as mere products of friendly obligation or economic need. Since the volume is compiled for scholars who read several languages, Beckett stipulates that these 'bits and pieces' be printed in the language of composition.

Like other scholars familiar with Beckett's criticism, I value it more than its author does. Like other scholars, too, I believe that the miscellany harbors an esthetic, but Beckett's criticism nevertheless resists a Procrustean coherence. Beckett himself observes (on Feuillerat's 'ordering' of Proust): '. . . a beautiful unity of tone and treatment would have, as it were, embalmed the whole'. To avoid embalming the whole, we should savor Beckett's morsels in all their variety.

Although Beckett does not swerve from commitment to an art of questions, hesitations, explorations — its theory and practice — his expression erupts in provocative articles, disdainful reviews, reflective essays, searching letters, and rare lyrical homage. To invite continuous reading, I have grouped the material by subject: 1) more or less formal esthetics, 2) literary criticism, 3) art criticism. By way of introduction, however, I prefer to move in stricter chronology: 1) Beckett's early mannered but nevertheless discerning perceptions; 2) commissions for periodical publication; 3) explicit exploration of the artist's calling; 4) postwar art criticism; 5) published commentary on his own work.

* * *

1) *The Young Scholar*

Today we are not surprised that Beckett was drawn to two modern giants, Joyce and Proust, but they did not tower so high in the late 1920s, and Beckett's essays were lucky assignments. In 1928, when he left Dublin as an exchange student to Paris, Beckett met a Joyce who was anxious to publicize *Work in Progress* by a volume of laudatory essays. Since Beckett had studied Italian, and particularly Dante, at Trinity College, Joyce proposed that the 22-year old student trace *Work*'s debt to the Italian trinity of Dante, Bruno, and Vico. Obligingly, Beckett read Vico's *Scienza Nuova*, which he then analyzed so acutely that, decades later, he is cited in Vico bibliographies. More strikingly original are the parallels Beckett draws between Dante and Joyce — unlikely to be cited in Dante bibliographies.

Of particular relevance in the context of this volume is Beckett's much quoted declaration: 'Literary criticism is not book-keeping', and he proceeds to prove that *Samuel Beckett's* literary criticism is closer to dart-shooting (against Benedetto Croce on Vico and against all philistines on Joyce). But Beckett could also register admiration, and he praises Vico's concern with myth, language, and poetry in his 'new science'. Although Beckett dutifully points to the importance of Viconian structure in *Work in Progress*, his primary enthusiasm is language as form *and* content. And it is by language that Beckett yokes Joyce to Dante, for he contends that they both invented a distinctive ideolect, spoken by no one. However, Beckett closes *Dante . . . Bruno . Vico . . Joyce* on metaphysics rather than language, and on contrast rather than resemblance. Unlike Dante, Beckett's Joyce views this earth as Purgatory, and any two opposing principles can make the purgatorial world go round. Beckett's Joyce thus erects an esthetic structure on the ancient framework of religious ethics. The new closed system is amoral and arbitrary.

Young Beckett's rapport with Proust was less personal and more profound. Dead in 1922, when Beckett was 16, Proust was little read at the beginning of the socially conscious 1930s. Beckett himself had only dipped into Proust before receiving a contract from an English publisher. After two Paris years as *lecteur* at the prestigious Ecole Normale Supérieure — two years spent in a more Bohemian than academic fashion — Beckett devoted the summer of 1930 to careful perusal of *A la recherche du temps perdu*. His detailed analysis of themes and texture still serves the Proust tyro, and his translations of key passages improve on the Scott Moncrieff version of 1922. Although Beckett dislikes the monograph and will not permit its translation into French, *Proust* was a modest success, both critically and commercially.

Subduing the polemical tone of the Joyce essay, the budding scholar refers in *Proust* to such tried and true critical pigeonholes as Romanticism, Symbolism, Relativism, Impressionism — all resistant to Realism, the dominant mode of the period. Beckett never explicitly compares Proust to Joyce, but he approves of both writers for fusing form and content. The admiring Joyce disciple assumes critical distance from Proust who is called 'the garrulous old dowager of the letters' who can repeat himself 'ad nauseam'. As the monograph proceeds, however, Beckett's appreciation grows for an author with whom he shares fundamental tenets — 'primacy of instinctive perception', style as vision more than technique, 'an art that is perfectly intelligible and perfectly inexplicable'. It is, however, a minor note in *Proust* that will become Becktt's major critical chord — the mobile subject before an evanescent object.

Less than half the Joyce essay focuses on Joyce, but the whole Proust monograph is centered on Proust. Beckett's erudition is less obstreperous — proper names, artistic movements, untranslated Spanish and Italian. Many pages look as though the paragraph had never been invented. *Proust* has been called portentous, but the prose can be defended as Beckett himself defended Proust: 'The complaint that it is an involved style, full of periphrasis, obscure and impossible to follow, has no foundation whatsoever.' Beckett respects academic form by occasional footnotes, but he refers to no earlier Proust critics, and he throws unscholarly darts at such contemporaries as Cocteau, France, Gide. Beckett's *Proust* nevertheless fits the academic mould more snugly than he himself could do, once he returned to Dublin to teach at Trinity College.

It was probably at this time that he played a trick on the

Moden Language Society of Dublin — the kind of trick that Parisians would recognize as a *canular normalien*. To a learned society, Beckett read — in French — a learned paper on a Toulouse author Jean du Chas, founder of Concentrism. Chas and his Concentrism, however, were pure fiction, having been invented by Beckett to mock pedantry, elsewhere called 'loutishness of learning'.

Beckett resigned from Trinity at the end of 1931, terminating his brief academic career. For years afterwards — until the unexpected success of *Waiting for Godot* — he was an author who did not earn sufficient income to sustain him. In 1932, back in Paris, he began his first novel *Dream of Fair to Middling Woman*, even while doubting the viability of the novel form. Esthetics therefore infiltrate the picaresque account of the amatory adventures of his protagonist Belacqua. Beckett's anonymous narrator fabricates a *chinoiserie* that attempts to confine fiction in a closed system, only to find that his characters refuse enclosure. Most recalcitrant is Belacqua, himself a wouldbe writer who espouses silence. Belacqua meditates on the book he would like to write, comparing it to Beethoven's music with its 'punctuation of dehiscence'. Belacqua forecasts Beckett's *Trilogy* in his fantasy of a rigorously structured book that looks improvised. *Dream* itself is the obverse — innocent of structure but guilty of mannered prose.

In the same year as *Dream*, 1932, Beckett signed a manifesto published in *transition* — 'Poetry is Vertical' — but he had no part of its composition.

2) *The Journalist*

Beckett revised the adventures of Belacqua into a series of stories which were published in 1934 in London as *More Pricks Than Kicks*. On the strength of this achievement and with the help of friends, he hoped to earn money in literary journalism. His few reviews are corrosive, pouring scorn on a Mozart biographer, an academic Proustian, a translator of Rilke, a Catholic interpreter of Dante, and almost all contemporary Irish poets. (His most withering piece — on Irish censorship — languished unpublished.) Beckett's rare praise is reserved for the 'knockabouts' of Sean O'Casey, the 'Spartan maieutics' of Ezra Pound, and the (unremarkable) verse of his Irish friends Brian

Coffey, Denis Devlin, and Thomas McGreevy.

Miscellaneous pieces though they are, the reviews are similar in assurance, erudition, and lucidity — a continuation of the *Proust* tone. The longest review 'Recent Irish Poetry' expands on the *Proust* motif of instability of subject and object. Beckett divides contemporary Irish poets into 'antiquarians' and those who are aware of a 'rupture of the lines of communication' because of the breakdown of subject and/or object. He cites no Irish poet with such awareness; instead, he praises an Irish painter, Jack Yeats, and an Anglo-American poet, T.S. Eliot.

By the mid-1930s Beckett abandoned literary journalism for creation. In 1935 his collection of verse *Echo's Bones* appeared in Paris. By 1936 he had completed *Murphy*, his most traditional novel, but it was still unpublished when he returned from London to Dublin, where he reviewed a book by the painter Jack Yeats. Beckett hails Yeats' *Amaranthers* for its discontinuities and its lack of those staples of fiction — reportage, allegory, symbol, and satire. In celebrating the imagination, Yeats traces a development that Beckett himself will later claim: 'You begin to stop emptying your heads, every time they begin to fill with thoughts, and then you will begin to think, and then you will stop thinking and begin to talk. . . . And then you will stop talking and begin to fancy, and then you will stop fancying and begin to imagine.'

3) *The Esthetic Explorer*

For a time Beckett put aside his own art to ponder its direction. Uniquely explicit, a letter of 1937 reveals more of his artistic credo than any other critical document. To a German acquaintance who had asked him to translate some verse, Beckett expressed a desire for 'a literature of the unword'. Condemning language as a 'veil that must be torn apart in order to get at the things (or the Nothingness) behind it', Beckett castigates literature for lagging behind the other arts that critically appraise their respective mediums. He yearns for silence to bore holes in language, and he contrasts this as yet unwritten literature with the Joycean 'apotheosis of the word'. Gertrude Stein might be a more suitable guide, but she is 'in love with her vehicle'. While waiting for his own vehicle, Beckett admits to amusing himself, as in this German letter, by inadvertently sinning against a foreign language as he hopes deliberately to sin against his own. Beckett's German letter is thus a declaration of creation through decreation.

That same year, 1937, Beckett reviewed poems by his friend Denis Devlin, quoting copiously and praising fulsomely. Although the Devlin quotations do not support Beckett's critical stance, that stance is firm: he sides with the self against society, the microcosm against the macrocosm, depth against surface, intuition against intellect. Moreover, art appears to him to be, through hesitation and interrogation, the expression of a need. The reviewer's role is to testify to the nature of the need.

Within a year Beckett moved to Paris and wrote in French — verse and another major esthetic statement, 'Les Deux besoins'. As though suddenly aware of the paradox of a 'literature of the unword', he groped toward the unword through a density of words. Thus, Beckett does not explicitly name the titular needs out of which the work of art is born, but he exalts art as the only path to knowledge about the self. The drive to such knowledge, a need, is countered by a need denying such knowledge, and out of their conflict/synthesis arises the work of art. In Lawrence Harvey's fine summary, the artist is poised 'in delicate balance between the need for privation and the need for fulfillment; and the synthesis of thesis and antithesis comes in the third condition, the need to make.' Beckett summons geometry to situate the contemporary artist; the relation of side and hypotenuse of a triangle (already pondered in *Murphy*) is an irrational number, a metaphor for the artist's 'hell of irreason'. Despatching science, theology, and Cartesian dualism, Beckett envisages an art riddled with questions rather than sealed off in solutions. And the whole is phrased in question-provoking French. Beckett mirrors the difficulty of the thought or artefact in the difficulty of his critical essay — not without grace.

4) *The Art Critic*

When Beckett moved to Paris in 1938, he made friends with visual artists as well as writers — Giacometti, Hayter, the van Velde brothers, and, later in Roussillon, Hayden. Still uncertain of his income at the end of World War II, Beckett accepted two assignments in art criticism. Perhaps this venture was triggered by a last favor to his friend McGreevy, whose book on Jack Yeats was published during Beckett's brief postwar visit to Dublin. Entitled 'MacGreevy [sic] on Yeats', the review is divided into three parts. First Beckett points out that McGreevy wrote his Yeats monograph in 1938 but could not find a publisher, in spite of his critical competence. The rest of the essay sets 'The National Painter' against 'The Artist'. McGreevy's view of Jack Yeats is subsumed under the first heading, Beckett's under the second. Beckett summarizes McGreevy's nationalist portrait of Jack Yeats, the more sharply to diverge from it.

Beckett's artist is above 'local accident' or 'local substance', and he groups Yeats with 'the great of our time, Kandinsky and Klee, Ballmer and Bram van Velde, Rouault and Braque' (craftily bracketing two unknowns by acknowledged celebrities). After sketching typical Yeats scenes, Beckett affirms that the artist reveals an invisible world through his 'notations'. The last words of the review ascribe no more sense to an inward than an outward artistic search, and yet appreciation of an inner drive will seep into Beckett's criticism and creation.

No sooner did Beckett leave Dublin for postwar France than he wrote (on commission) a long essay to coincide with exhibitions of painting by the virtually unknown van Velde brothers. That piece is unique in examining, almost dramatizing, the predicament of the non-professional art-lover, who is assaulted by the verbiage of art criticism. A third of Beckett's article is over before he reaches the painting of the two Dutch brothers whose vision is similar but whose paintings contrast.

'L'art adore les sauts', Beckett announces late in the essay, and his criticism also adores leaps — from viewer to reviewer to painting personified, then back to the poor viewer to whom the piece is dedicated. After generalizing about the painting of the dissimilar brothers (but without naming a single painting), Beckett acclaims critical art i.e. an art that is critical of its objects, methods, goals, and criticism. He then leaps back to the van Veldes and their obsession with representing change. Another leap lands him on the 'human' and similar extra-esthetic criteria by which contemporary art has the misfortune to be judged. In that context the van Veldes would be stoned, or perhaps merely hooted down. Many stupid things will be written about these two artist brothers, Beckett predicts, and he declares it an honor to lead the list.

Unlike Beckett's English journalism, the French counterpart wears its learning lightly, with witty sallies and exposed clichés. Although his van Velde interpretations are idiosyncratic, they are also perceptive. They testify to his continued preoccupation with the rupture of relation between subject and object, but the continuation is almost parenthetical to a subtextual plea to the art-lover to trust his eyes rather than words, which this essay contains in abundance.

As all Beckett scholars know, 1946–1950 was his most fertile period, but it was not until the mid-1950s that he could live on his royalties. Even during the momentum of writing the *Trilogy*, he accepted odd assignments, and, again on commission, he continued his defense of an art critical of its object. 'Peintres de l'empêchement' (1948) was originally entitled 'Le Nouvel objet'. Aware of repeating himself on the breakdown of the subject-object relation, Beckett weaves that repetition into critical irony. With tongue in cheek, he maintains that constant statement and restatement of opinions about painting can free one from looking at individual paintings.

Beckett sums up three possibilities for the modern artist: 1) to be an antiquarian in the old subject-object tradition, 2) to risk a few uncertain steps toward a new tradition, or 3) to discover in the absence of traditional relation and object a new relation and object. Immersed as Beckett was in his own exploration of a new relation and object — an immersion of élan — he ends the essay with comparable élan at the third way of art.

A year later élan is submerged in *Three Dialogues*, Beckett's best-known art criticism. Requested rather than commissioned, the piece is ascribed to Samuel Beckett and Georges Duthuit, the editor of the postwar *transition*. However, Beckett alone wrote the dialogues that 'merely reflect, very freely, the many conversations we had at that time about painters and painting.' To Martin Esslin, Beckett remarked that he wrote the talks *up* rather than *down*. Like Brecht's *Messingkauf Dialogues*, those of Beckett are dramatic enough to perform.

The scene is readily imaginable — street, cafe, or gallery where two art critics, B and D, air their differences. Although Beckett does not refer to his most recent essay on impediment-painting, he selects three painters who illustrate the three possibilities of modern art: Tal Coat (and, incidentally, Matisse), despite prodigious painterly talent, is an antiquarian in his subject-object relation; Masson, influenced by the Orient, yearns for a void, but through that very yearning flaunts his possession of space; the third way of passive acceptance of crisis belongs to Bram van Velde (with Geer nowhere in sight). For 'object' Beckett substitutes the word 'occasion', which seems less stable and solid. In Beckett's radical esthetic of failure, it is no longer sufficient to replace the old relation and occasion with new ones. It is unsatisfactory to convert 'fidelity to failure' into 'a new occasion'. Bram van Velde simply paints, without relation and without waving the banner of his failure. Or at least that is B's 'fancy' of what Bram van Velde does. B flees from the scene without presuming to pronounce what van Velde 'more than likely' does. B's last words undermine all he has said: 'Yes, yes, I am mistaken, I am mistaken.' — circling round to the Descartes of Beckett's 1930 *Whoroscope*: 'Fallor, ergo sum!'

Three Dialogues is so well worn as a springboard for Beckett interpretation that one may recall D's injunction to B: '. . . the subject under discussion is not yourself'. Nevertheless, Beckett's hyperawareness of an unsteady eye on an evanescent occasion is the fulcrum of his recent (1982) fiction *Mal vu mal dit*. In his 1952 tribute to Henri Hayden, Beckett phrases it as 'a self, such as it is, and an impregnable nature'. But the man-painter paints.

Beckett's other brief tributes to artist friends — Bram van Velde again, Jack Yeats again, Henri Hayden again, and Avigdor Arikha — convey his appreciation of their respective 'needs'. One might describe these pieces as lyrics of criticism, and the two he translated display his matchless skill in that craft.

5) *The Self-Critic*

Although refusing interviews, Beckett has chatted informally with all too many people who have rushed into print. Only in private letters has he *written* about his own writing, and since their publication is scattered, they are here reprinted.

*   *   *

Apart from Beckett's criticism is another disjectum, 'Human Wishes', a fragmentary scene of 1937. It was left at my Paris hotel when I did not even know of its existence, and only recently has Beckett consented to its publication, fulfilling a few human wishes.

Finally, the generosity of Samuel Beckett is happily infectious, and in the editing of this volume I am indebted to James Acheson, Linda Ben-Zvi, Martin Esslin, Martha Fehsenfeld, Stan Gontarski, Jan Hokenson, James Knowlson, James Mays, Dougald McMillan, and David Robertson, whom it is a pleasure to thank warmly. I also acknowledge assistance from Research funds at the University of California, Davis. Above all, I am beholden to Samuel Beckett for overcoming his reluctance to see publication of these delectable disjecta.

RUBY COHN

Part I

Essays at Esthetics

1.   Dante . . . Bruno . Vico . . Joyce

The danger is in the neatness of identifications. The conception of Philosophy and Philology as a pair of nigger minstrels out of the Teatro dei Piccoli is soothing, like the contemplation of a carefully folded ham-sandwich. Giambattista Vico himself could not resist the attractiveness of such coincidence of gesture. He insisted on complete identification between the philosophical abstraction and the empirical illustration, thereby annulling the absolutism of each conception — hoisting the real unjustifiably clear of its dimensional limits, temporalizing that which is extratemporal. And now here am I, with my handful of abstractions, among which notably: a mountain, the coincidence of contraries, the inevitability of cyclic evolution, a system of Poetics, and the prospect of self-extension in the world of Mr Joyce's *Work in Progress*. There is the temptation to treat every concept like 'a bass dropt neck fust in till a bung crate', and make a really tidy job of it. Unfortunately such an exactitude of application would imply distortion in one of two directions. Must we wring the neck of a certain system in order to stuff it into a contemporary pigeon-hole, or modify the dimensions of that pigeon-hole for the satisfaction of the analogymongers? Literary criticism is not book-keeping.

. . . .

Giambattista Vico was a practical roundheaded Neapolitan. It pleases Croce to consider him as a mystic, essentially speculative, '*disdegnoso dell' empirismo*'. It is a surprising interpretation, seeing that more than three-fifths of his *Scienza Nuova* is concerned with empirical investigation. Croce opposes him to the reformative materialistic school of Ugo Grozio, and absolves him from the utilitarian preoccupations of Hobbes, Spinoza, Locke, Bayle and Machiavelli. All this cannot be swallowed without protest. Vico defines Providence as: '*una mente spesso diversa ed alle volte tutta contraria e sempre superiore ad essi fini particolari che essi uomini si avevano proposti; dei quali fini ristretti fatti mezzi per servire a fini più ampi, gli ha sempre adoperati per conservare l'umana generazione in questa terra.'* What could be more definitely utilitarianism? His treatment of the origin and functions of poetry, language and myth, as will appear later, is as far removed from the mystical as it is possible to imagine. For our immediate purpose, however, it matters little whether we consider him as a mystic or as a scientific investigator; but there are no two ways about considering him as an *innovator*. His division of the development of human society into three ages: Theocratic, Heroic, Human (civilized), with a corresponding classification of language: Hieroglyphic (sacred), Metaphorical (poetic), Philosophical (capable of abstraction and generalization), was by no means new, although it must have appeared so to his contemporaries. He derived this convenient classification from the Egyptians, via Herodotus. At the same time it is impossible to deny the originality with which he applied and developed its implications. His exposition of the ineluctable circular progression of Society was completely new, although the germ of it was contained in Giordano Bruno's treatment of identified contraries. But it is in Book 2, described by himself as *'tutto il corpo . . . la chiave maestra . . . dell' opera'*, that appears the unqualified originality of his mind; here he evolved a theory of the origins of poetry and language, the significance of myth, and the nature of barbaric civilization that must have appeared nothing less than an impertinent outrage against tradition. These two aspects of Vico have their reverberations, their reapplications — without, however, receiving the faintest explicit illustration — in *Work in Progress*.

It is first necessary to condense the thesis of Vico, the scientific historian. In the beginning was the thunder: the thunder set free Religion, in its most objective and unphilosophical form — idolatrous animism: Religion produced Society, and the first social men were the cave-dwellers, taking refuge from a passionate Nature: this primitive family life receives its first impulse towards development from the arrival of terrified vagabonds: admitted, they are the first slaves: growing stronger, they exact agrarian concessions, and a despotism has evolved into a primitive feudalism: the cave becomes a city, and the feudal system a democracy: then an anarchy: this is corrected by a return to monarchy: the last stage is a tendency towards interdestruction: the nations are dispersed, and the Phoenix of Society arises out of their ashes. To this six-termed social progression corresponds a six-termed progression of human motives: necessity, utility, convenience, pleasure, luxury, abuse of luxury: and their incarnate manifestations: Polyphemus, Achilles, Caesar and Alexander, Tiberius, Caligula and Nero. At this point Vico applies Bruno — though he takes very good care not to say so — and proceeds from rather arbitrary data to philosophical abstraction. There is no difference, says Bruno, between the smallest possible chord and the smallest possible arc, no difference between the infinite circle and the straight line. The maxima and minima of particular contraries are one and indifferent. Minimal heat equals minimal cold. Consequently transmutations are circular. The principle (minimum) of one contrary takes its movement from the principle (maximum) of one another. Therefore not only do the minima coincide with the minima, the maxima with the maxima, but the minima with the maxima in the succession of transmutations. Maximal speed is a state of rest. The maximum of corruption and the minimum of generation are identical: in principle, corruption is generation. And all things are ultimately identified with God, the universal monad, Monad of monads. From these considerations Vico evolved a Science and Philosophy of History. It may be an amusing exercise to take an historical figure, such as Scipio, and label him No. 3; it is of no ultimate importance. What is of ultimate importance is the recognition that the passage from Scipio to Caesar is as inevitable as the passage from Caesar to Tiberius, since the flowers of corruption in Scipio and Caesar are the seeds of vitality in Caesar and Tiberius. Thus we have the spectacle of a human progression that depends for its movement on individuals, and which at the same time is independent of individuals in virtue of what appears to be a preordained cyclicism. It follows that History is neither to be considered as a formless structure, due exclusively to the achievements of individual agents, nor as possessing reality apart from and independent of them, accomplished behind their backs in spite of them, the work of some superior force, variously known as Fate, Chance, Fortune, God. Both these views, the materialistic and the transcendental, Vico rejects in favour of the rational. Individuality is the concretion of universality, and every individual action is at the same time superindividual. The individual and the universal cannot be considered as distinct from each other. History, then, is not the result of Fate or Chance — in both cases the individual would be separated from his product — but the result of a Necessity that is not Fate, of a Liberty that is not Chance (compare Dante's 'yoke of liberty'). This force he called Divine Providence, with his tongue, one feels, very much in his cheek. And it is to this Providence that we must trace the three institutions common to every society: Church, Marriage, Burial. This is not Bossuet's Providence, transcendental and miraculous, but immanent and the stuff itself of human life, working by natural means. Humanity is its work in itself. God acts on her, but by means of her. Humanity is divine, but no man is divine. This social and historical classification is clearly adapted by Mr Joyce as a structural convenience — or inconvenience. His position is in no way a philosophical one. It is the detached attitude of Stephen Dedalus in *Portrait of the Artist* . . . who describes Epictetus to the Master of Studies as 'an old gentleman who said that the soul is very like a bucketful of water.' The lamp is more important than the lamp-lighter. By structural I do not only mean a bold outward division, a bare skeleton for the housing of material. I mean the endless substantial variations on these three beats, and interior intertwining of these three themes into a decoration of arabesques — decoration and more than decoration. Part 1 is a mass of past shadow, corresponding therefore to Vico's first human institution, Religion, or to his Theocratic age, or simply to an abstraction — Birth. Part 2 is the lovegame of the children, corresponding to the second institution, Marriage, or to the Heroic age, or to an abstraction — Maturity. Part 3 is passed in sleep, corresponding to the third institution, Burial, or to the Human age, or to an abstraction — Corruption. Part 4 is the day beginning again, and corresponds to Vico's Providence, or to an abstraction — Generation. Mr Joyce does not take birth for granted, as Vico seems to have done. So much for the dry bones. The consciousness that there is a great deal of the unborn infant in the lifeless octogenarian, and a great deal of both in the man at the apogee of his life's curve, removes all the stiff interexclusiveness that is often the danger in neat

22

construction. Corruption is not excluded from Part 1 nor maturity from Part 3. The four 'lovedroyd curdinals' are presented on the same plane — 'his element curdinal numen and his enement curdinal marrying and his epulent curdinal weisswasch and his eminent curdinal Kay o' Kay!' There are numerous references to Vico's four human institutions — Providence counting as one! 'A good clap, a fore wedding, a bad wake, tell hell's well': 'their weatherings and their marryings and their buryings and their natural selections': 'the lightning look, the birding cry, awe from the grave, ever-flowing on our times': 'by four hands of forethought the first babe of reconcilement is laid in its last cradle of hume sweet hume.'

Apart from this emphasis on the tangible conveniences common to Humanity, we find frequent expressions of Vico's insistence on the inevitable character of every progression — or retrogression: 'The Vico road goes round to meet where terms begin. Still onappealed to by the cycles and onappalled by the recoursers, we feel all serene, never you fret, as regards our dutyful cask. . . . before there was a man at all in Ireland there was a lord at Lucan. We only wish everyone was as sure of anything in this watery world as we are of everything in the newlywet fellow that's bound to follow. . . .' 'The efferfresh-painted livy in beautific repose upon the silence of the dead from Pharoph the next first down to ramescheckles the last bust thing.' 'In fact, under the close eyes of the inspectors the traits featuring the chiaroscuro coalesce, their contrarieties eliminated, in one stable somebody similarly as by the providential warring of heartshaker with housebreaker and of dramdrinker against freethinker our social something bowls along bumpily, experiencing a jolting series of prearranged disappointments, down the long lane of (it's as semper as oxhousehumper) generations, more generations and still more generations' — this last a case of Mr Joyce's rare subjectivism. In a word, here is all humanity circling with fatal monotony about the Providential fulcrum — the 'convoy wheeling enciruling abound the gigantig's lifetree'. Enough has been said, or at least enough has been suggested, to show how Vico is substantially present in the *Work in Progress*. Passing to the Vico of the Poetics we hope to establish an even more striking, if less direct, relationship.

Vico rejected the three popular interpretations of the poetic spirit, which considered poetry as either an ingenious popular expression of philosophical conceptions, or an amusing social diversion, or an exact science within the research of everyone in possession of the recipe. Poetry, he says, was born of curiosity, daughter of ignorance. The first men had to create matter by the force of their imagination, and 'poet' means 'creator'. Poetry was the first operation of the human mind, and without it thought could not exist. Barbarians, incapable of analysis and abstraction, must use their fantasy to explain what their reasons cannot comprehend. Before articulation comes song; before abstract terms, metaphors. The figurative character of the oldest poetry must be regarded, not as sophisticated confectionery, but as evidence of a poverty-stricken vocabulary and of a disability to achieve abstraction. Poetry is essentially the antithesis of Metaphysics: Metaphysics purge the mind of the senses and cultivate the disembodiment of the spiritual; Poetry is all passion and feeling and animates the inanimate; Metaphysics are most perfect when most concerned with universals; Poetry, when most concerned with particulars. Poets are the sense, philosophers the intelligence of humanity. Considering the Scholastics' axiom: *'niente è nell'intelletto che prima non sia nel senso'*, it follows that poetry is a prime condition of philosophy and civilization. The primitive animistic movement was a manifestation of the *'forma poetica dello spirito'*.

His treatment of the origin of language proceeds along similar lines. Here again he rejected the materialistic and transcendental views; the one declaring that language was nothing but a polite and conventional symbolism; the other, in desperation, describing it as a gift from the Gods. As before, Vico is the rationalist, aware of the natural and inevitable growth of language. In its first dumb form, language was gesture. If a man wanted to say 'sea', he pointed to the sea. With the spread of animism this gesture was replaced by the word: 'Neptune'. He directs our attention to the fact that every need of life, natural, moral and economic, has its verbal expression in one or other of the 30,000 Greek divinities. This is Homer's 'language of the Gods'. Its evolution through poetry to a highly civilized vehicle, rich in abstract and technical terms, was as little fortuitous as the evolution of society itself. Words have their progressions as well as social phases. 'Forest-cabin-village-city-academy' is one rough progression. Another: 'mountain-plain-riverbank'. And every word expands with psychological inevitability. Take the Latin word: 'Lex'.

1.   Lex = Crop of acorns.
2.   Ilex = Tree that produces acorns.
3.   Legere = To gather.
4.   Aquilex = He that gathers the waters.
5.   Lex = Gathering together of peoples, public assembly.
6.   Lex = Law.
7.   Legere = To gather together letters into a word, to read.

The root of any word whatsoever can be traced back to some pre-lingual symbol. This early inability to abstract the general from the particular produced the Type-names. It is the child's mind over again. The child extends the names of the first familiar objects to other strange objects in which he is conscious of some analogy. The first men, unable to conceive the abstract idea of 'poet' or 'hero', named every hero after the first hero, every poet after the first poet. Recognizing this custom of designating a number of individuals by the names of their prototypes, we can explain various classical and mythological mysteries. Hermes is the prototype of the Egyptian inventor: so for Romulus, the great law-giver, and Hercules, the Greek hero: so for Homer. Thus Vico asserts the spontaneity of language and denies the dualism of poetry and language. Similarly, poetry is the foundation of writing. When language consisted of gesture, the spoken and written were identical. Hieroglyphics, or sacred language, as he calls it, were not the invention of philosophers for the mysterious expression of profound thought, but the common necessity of primitive peoples. Convenience only begins to assert itself at a far more advanced stage of civilization, in the form of alphabetism. Here Vico, implicitly at least, distinguishes between writing and direct expression. In such direct expression, form and content are inseparable. Examples are the medals of the Middle Ages, which bore no inscription and were a mute testimony to the feebleness of conventional alphabetic writing: and the flags of our own day. As with Poetry and Language, so with Myth. Myth, according to Vico, is neither an allegorical expression of general philosophical axioms (Conti, Bacon), nor a derivative from particular peoples, as for instance the Hebrews or Egyptians, nor yet the work of isolated poets, but an historical statement of fact, of actual contemporary phenomena, actual in the sense that they were created out of necessity by primitive minds, and firmly believed. Allegory implies a threefold intellectual operation: the construction of a message of general significance, the preparation of a fabulous form, and an exercise of considerable technical difficulty in uniting the two, an operation totally beyond the reach of the primitive mind. Moreover, if we consider the myth as being essentially allegorical, we are not obliged to accept the form in which it is cast as a statement of fact. But we know that the actual creators of these myths gave full credence to their face-value. Jove was no symbol: he was terribly real. It was precisely their superficial metaphorical character that made them intelligible to people incapable of receiving anything more abstract than the plain record of objectivity.

Such is a painful exposition of Vico's dynamic treatment of Language, Poetry and Myth. He may still appear as a mystic to some: if so, a mystic that rejects the transcendental in every shape and form as a factor in human development, and whose Providence is not divine enough to do without the cooperation of Humanity.

On turning to the *Work in Progress* we find that the mirror is not so convex. Here is direct expression — pages and pages of it. And if you don't understand it, Ladies and Gentlemen, it is because you are too decadent to receive it. You are not satisfied unless form is so strictly divorced from content that you can comprehend the one almost without bothering to read the other. The rapid skimming and absorption of the scant cream of sense is made possible by what I may call a continuous process of copious intellectual salivation. The form that is an arbitrary and independent phenomenon can fulfil no higher function than that of stimulus for a tertiary or quartary conditioned reflex of dribbling comprehension. When Miss Rebecca West clears her decks for a sorrowful deprecation of the Narcisstic element in Mr Joyce by the purchase of 3 hats, one feels that she might very well wear her bib at all her intellectual banquets, or alternatively, assert a more noteworthy control over her salivary glands than is possible for Monsieur Pavlov's unfortunate dogs. The title of this book is a good example of a form carrying a strict inner determination. It should be proof against the usual volley of cerebral sniggers: and it may suggest to some a dozen incredulous Joshuas prowling around the Queen's Hall, springing their tuning-forks lightly against finger-nails that have not yet been refined out of existence. Mr Joyce has a word to say to you on the subject: 'Yet to concentrate solely on the literal sense or even the psychological content of any document to the sore neglect of the enveloping facts themselves circumstantiating it is just as harmful; etc.' And another: 'Who in his heart doubts either that the facts of feminine clothiering are there all the time or that the feminine fiction, stranger than the facts, is there also at the same time, only a little to the rere? Or that one may be separated from the other? Or that both may be contemplated simultaneously? Or that each may be taken up in turn and considered apart from the other?'

Here form *is* content, content *is* form. You complain that this stuff is not written in English. It is not written at all. It is not to be read — or rather it is not only to be read. It is to be looked at and listened to. His writing is not *about* something; *it is that something itself.* (A fact that has been grasped by an eminent English novelist and historian whose work is in complete opposition to Mr Joyce's.) When the sense is sleep, the words go to sleep. (See the end of *Anna Livia*.) When the sense is dancing, the words dance. Take the passage at the end of Shaun's pastoral: 'To stirr up love's young fizz I tilt with this bridle's cup champagne, dimming douce from her peepair of hide-seeks tight squeezed on my snowybreasted and while my pearlies in their sparkling wisdom are nippling her bubblets I swear (and let you swear) by the bumper round of my poor old snaggletooth's solidbowel I ne'er will prove I'm untrue to (theare!) you liking so long as my hole looks. Down.' The language is drunk. The very words are tilted and effervescent. How can we qualify this general esthetic vigilance without which we cannot hope to snare the sense which is for ever rising to the surface of the form and becoming the form itself? St Augustine puts us on the track of a word with his '*intendere*', Dante has: '*Donne ch'avete intelletto d'amore*', and *Voi che, intendendo, il terzo ciel movete*'; but his '*intendere*' suggests a strictly intellectual operation. When an Italian says to-day '*Ho inteso*', he means something between '*Ho udito*' and '*Ho capito*', a sensuous untidy art of intellection. Perhaps 'apprehension' is the most satisfactory English word. Stephen says to Lynch: 'Temporal or spatial, the esthetic image is first luminously apprehended as selfbounded and selfcontained upon the immeasurable background of space or time which is not it. . . You apprehend its wholeness'. There is one point to make clear: the Beauty of *Work in Progress* is not presented in space alone, since its adequate apprehension depends as much on its visibility as on its audibility. There is a temporal as well as a spatial unity to be apprehended. Substitute 'and' for 'or' in the quotation, and it becomes obvious why it is as inadequate to speak of 'reading' *Work in Progress* as it would be extravagant to speak of 'apprehending' the work of the late Mr Nat Gould. Mr Joyce has desophisticated language. And it is worth while remarking that no language is so sophisticated as English. It is abstracted to death. Take the word 'doubt': it gives us hardly any sensuous suggestion of hesitancy, of the necessity for choice, of static irresolution. Whereas the German 'Zweifel' does, and, in lesser degree, the Italian 'dubitare'. Mr Joyce recognizes how inadequate 'doubt' is to express a state of extreme uncertainty, and replaces it by 'in twosome twiminds'. Nor is he by any means the first to recognize the importance of treating words as something more than mere polite symbols. Shakespeare uses fat, greasy words to express corruption: 'Duller shouldst thou be than the fat weed that rots itself in death on Lethe wharf'. We hear the ooze squelching all through Dickens's description of the Thames in *Great Expectations*. This writing that you find so obscure is a quintessential extraction of language and painting and gesture, with all the inevitable clarity of the old inarticulation. Here is the savage economy of hieroglyphics. Here words are not the polite contortions of 20th century printer's ink. They are alive. They elbow their way on to the page, and glow and blaze and fade and disappear. 'Brawn is my name and broad is my nature and I've breit on my brow and all's right with every feature and I'll brune this bird or Brown Bess's bung's gone bandy.' This is Brawn blowing with a light gust through the trees or Brawn passing with the sunset. Because the wind in the trees means as little to you as the evening prospect from the Piazzale Michelangiolo — though you accept them both because your non-acceptance would be of no significance, this little adventure of Brawn means nothing to you — and you do not accept it, even though here also your non-acceptance is of no significance. H. C. Earwigger, too, is not content to be mentioned like a shilling-shocker villain, and then dropped until the exigencies of the narrative require that he be again referred to. He continues to suggest himself for a couple of pages, by means of repeated permutations on his 'normative letters', as if to say: 'This is all about me, H. C. Earwigger: don't forget this is all about me!' This inner elemental vitality and corruption of expression imparts a furious restlessness to the form, which is admirably suited to the purgatorial aspect of the work. There is an endless verbal germination, maturation, putrefaction, the cyclic dynamism of the intermediate. This reduction of various expressive media to their primitive economic directness, and the fusion of these primal essences into an assimilated medium for the exteriorization of thought, is pure Vico, and Vico, applied to the problem of style. But Vico is reflected more explicitly than by a distillation of disparate poetic ingredients into a synthetical syrup. We notice that there is little or no attempt at subjectivism or abstraction, no attempt at metaphysical generalization. We are presented with a statement of the particular. It is the old myth: the girl on the dirt track, the two washerwomen on the banks of the river. And there is considerable animism: the mountain 'abhearing', the river puffing her old doudheen. (See the beautiful passage beginning: 'First she let her hair fall down and it flussed'.) We have Type-names: Isolde — any beautiful girl: Earwigger — Guinness's Brewery, the Wellington monument, the Phoenix Park, anything that occupies an extremely comfortable position between the two stools. Anna Livia herself, mother of Dublin, but no more the only mother than Zoroaster was the only oriental stargazer. 'Teems of times and happy returns. The same anew. Ordovico or viricordo. Anna was, Livia is, Plurabelle's to be. Northmen's thing made Southfolk's place, but howmultyplurators made eachone in person.' Basta! Vico and Bruno are here, and more substantially than would appear from this swift survey of the question. For the benefit of those who enjoy a parenthetical sneer, we would draw attention to the fact that when Mr Joyce's early pamphlet *The Day of Rabblement* appeared, the local philosophers were thrown into a state of some bewilderment by a reference in the first line to 'The Nolan'. They finally succeeded in identifying this mysterious individual with one of the obscurer ancient Irish kings. In the present work he appears frequently as 'Browne & Nolan', the name of a very remarkable Dublin Bookseller and Stationer.

To justify our title, we must move North, *'Sovra'l bel fiume d'Arno alla gran villa'* . . . . Between *'colui per lo cui verso — il meonio cantor non è più solo'* and the 'still to-day insufficiently malestimated notesnatcher, Shem the Penman', there exists considerable circumstantial similarity. They both saw how worn out and threadbare was the conventional language of cunning literary artificers, both rejected an approximation to a universal language. If English is not yet so definitely a polite necessity as Latin was in the Middle Ages, at least one is justified in declaring that its position in relation to other European languages is to a great extent that of mediaeval Latin to the Italian dialects. Dante did not adopt the vulgar out of any kind of local jingoism nor out of any determination to assert the superiority of Tuscan to all its rivals as a form of spoken Italian. On reading his *De Vulgari Eloquentia* we are struck by his complete freedom from civic intolerance. He attacks the world's Portadownians: *'Nam quicumque tam obscenae rationis est, ut locum suae nationis delitosissimum credat esse sub sole, huic etiam proe cunctis propriam volgare licetur, idest maternam locutionem. Nos autem, cui mundus est patria . . . etc.'* When he comes to examine the dialects he finds Tuscan: *'turpissimum . . . fere omnes Tusci in suo turpiloquio obtusi . . . non restat in dubio quin aliud sit vulgare quod quaerimus quam quod attingit populus Tuscanorum.'* His conclusion is that the corruption common to all the dialects makes it impossible to select one rather than another as an adequate literary form, and that he who would write in the vulgar must assemble the purest elements from each dialect and construct a synthetic language that would at least possess more than a circumscribed local interest: which is precisely what he did. He did not write in Florentine any more than in Neapolitan. He wrote a vulgar that *could* have been spoken by an ideal Italian who had assimilated what was best in all the dialects of his country, but which in fact was certainly not spoken nor ever had been. Which disposes of the capital objection that might be made against this attractive parallel between Dante and Mr Joyce in the question of language, i.e. that at least Dante wrote what was being spoken in the streets of his own town, whereas no creature in heaven or earth ever spoke the language of

Work in Progress. It is reasonable to admit that an international phenomenon might be capable of speaking it, just as in 1300 none but an inter-regional phenomenon could have spoken the language of the Divine Comedy. We are inclined to forget that Dante's literary public was Latin that the form of his Poem was to be judged by Latin eyes and ears, by a Latin Esthetic intolerant of innovation, and which could hardly fail to be irritated by the substitution of *'Nel mezzo del cammin di nostra vita'* with its 'barbarous' directness for the suave elegance of: *'Ultima regna canam, fluido contermina mundo'*, just as English eyes and ears prefer: 'Smoking his favourite pipe in the sacred presence of ladies' to: 'Rauking his flavourite turfco in the smukking precincts of lydias'. Boccaccio did not jeer at the *'piedi sozzi'* of the peacock that Signora Alighieri dreamed about.

I find two well made caps in the *'Convivio'*, one to fit the collective noodle of the monodialectical arcadians whose fury is precipitated by a failure to discover 'innoce-free' in the concise Oxford Dictionary and who qualify as the 'ravings of a Bedlamite' the formal structure raised by Mr Joyce after years of patient and inspired labour: *'Questi sono da chiamare pecore e non uomini; chè se una pecora si gittasse da una ripa di mille passi, tutte l'altre le adrebbono dietro; e se una pecore a per alcuna cagione al passare d'una strada salta, tutte le altre saltano, eziando nulla veggendo da saltare. E io ne vidi già molte in un pozzo saltare, per una che dentro vi salto, forse credendo di saltare un muro.'* And the other for Mr Joyce, biologist in words: *'Questo* (formal innovation) *sarà luce nuova, sole nuovo, il quale sorgerà ore l'usato tramonterà e darà luce a coloro che sono in tenebre e in oscurità per lo usato sole che a loro non luce.'* And, lest he should pull it down over his eyes and laugh behind the peak, I translate *'in tenebre e in oscurità'* by 'bored to extinction'. (Dante makes a curious mistake speaking of the origin of language, when he rejects the authority of Genesis that Eve was the first to speak, when she addressed the Serpent. His incredulity is amusing: *'inconvenienter putatur tam egregium humani generis actum, vel prius quam a viro, foemina profluisse'*. But before Eve was born, 'the animals were given names by Adam', the man who 'first said goo to a goose'. Moreover it is explicitly stated that the choice of names was left entirely to Adam, so that there is not the slightest Biblical authority for the conception of language as a direct gift of God, any more than there is any intellectual authority for conceiving that we are indebted for the 'Concert' to the individual who used to buy paint for Giorgione.)

We know very little about the immediate reception accorded to Dante's mighty vindication of the 'vulgar', but we can form our own opinions when, two centuries later, we find Castiglione splitting more than a few hairs concerning the respective advantages of Latin and Italian, and Poliziano writing the dullest of dull Latin Elegies to justify his existence as the author of '*Orfeo*' and the '*Stanze*'. We may also compare, if we think it worth while, the storm of ecclesiastical abuse raised by Mr Joyce's work, and the treatment that the Divine Comedy must certainly have received from the same source. His Contemporary Holiness might have swallowed the crucifixion of '*lo sommo Giove*', and all it stood for, but he could scarcely have looked with favour on the spectacle of three of his immediate predecessors plunged head-foremost in the fiery stone of Malebolge, nor yet the identification of the Papacy in the mystical procession of Terrestrial Paradise with a '*puttana sciolta*'. The '*De Monarshia*' was burnt publicly under Pope Giovanni XXII at the instigation of Cardinal Beltrando and the bones of its author would have suffered the same fate but for the interference of an influential man of letters, Pino della Tosa. Another point of comparison is the preoccupation with the significance of numbers. The death of Beatrice inspired nothing less than a highly complicated poem dealing with the importance of the number 3 in her life. Dante never ceased to be obsessed by this number. Thus the poem is divided into three Cantiche, each composed of 33 Canti, and written in terza rima. Why, Mr Joyce seems to say, should there be four legs to a table, and four to a horse, and four seasons and four Gospels and four Provinces in Ireland? Why twelve Tables of the Law, and twelve Apostles and twelve months and twelve Napoleonic marshals and twelve men in Florence called Ottolenghi? Why should the Armistice be celebrated at the eleventh hour of the eleventh day of the eleventh month? He cannot tell you because he is not God Almighty, but in a thousand years he will tell you, and in the meantime must be content to know why horses have not five legs, nor three. He is conscious that things with a common numerical characteristic tend towards a very significant interrelationship. This preoccupation is freely translated in his present work, see the 'Question and Answer' chapter, and the Four speaking through the child's brain. They are the four winds as much as the four Provinces, and the four Episcopal Sees as much as either.

A last word about the Purgatories. Dante's is conical and consequently implies culmination. Mr Joyce's is spherical and excludes culmination. In the one there is an ascent from real vegetation — Ante-Purgatory, to ideal vegetation — Terrestrial Paradise: in the other there is no ascent and no ideal vegetation. In the one, absolute progression and a guaranteed consummation: in the other, flux — progression or retrogression, and an apparent consummation. In the one movement is unidirectional, and a step forward represents a net advance: in the other movement is non-directional — or multi-directional, and a step forward is, by definition, a step back. Dante's Terrestrial Paradise is the carriage entrance to a Paradise that is not terrestrial: Mr Joyce's Terrestrial Paradise is the tradesmen's entrance on to the sea-shore. Sin is an impediment to movement up the cone, and a condition of movement round the sphere. In what sense, then, is Mr Joyce's work purgatorial? In the absolute absence of the Absolute. Hell is the static lifelessness of unrelieved viciousness. Paradise the static lifelessness of unrelieved immaculation. Purgatory a flood of movement and vitality released by the conjunction of these two elements. There is a continuous purgatorial process at work, in the sense that the vicious circle of humanity is being achieved, and this achievement depends on the recurrent predomination of one of two broad qualities. No resistance, no eruption, and it is only in Hell and Paradise that there are no eruptions, that there can be none, need be none. On this earth that is Purgatory, Vice and Virtue — which you may take to mean any pair of large contrary human factors — must in turn be purged down to spirits of rebelliousness. Then the dominant crust of the Vicious or Virtuous sets, resistance is provided, the explosion duly takes place and the machine proceeds. And no more than this; neither prize nor penalty; simply a series of stimulants to enable the kitten to catch its tail. And the partially purgatorial agent? The partially purged.

2. Le Concentrisme

Monsieur

Vous êtes le premier à vous intéresser à cet imbécile. Voici tout ce que j'en sais: j'ai fait sa connaissance ou, plus exactement, il m'a imposé cette incommodité, la veille de sa mort, à Marseille. Il s'est cramponné à moi dans un sombre bistrot où, à cette époque, j'avais l'excellente habitude d'aller me soûler deux fois par semaine. 'Vous avez l'air' me dit-il 'suffisament idiot pour m'inspirer une confiance extrême. Enfin' poursuivit-il — (je ne change rien à ses logogriphes) — 'enfin et pour la première fois je tombe sur un animal qui, si j'ose en croire mes yeux, est totalement et idéalement dépourvu d'intelligence, plongé dans une divine et parfaite nullité.' Il s'interrompit, se découvrit, et puis, d'une voix vibrante: 'Je vous embrasse, mon frère!' s'écria-t-il. Je le repoussai vivement. Il faillit tomber, pâlit, et se mit à tousser d'une façon si douleureuse que je ne pus m'empêcher de regretter la violence de mon geste. Mais il se reprit bientôt et m'adressa de nouveau, maintenant d'une voix à peine perceptible.
'Monsieur' dit-il, 'permettez-vous que je vous pose une question?'
'Faites, Monsieur', lui dis-je, froidement.
'Seriez-vous de Toulouse, par hasard?'
'Oui, Monsieur.' Il tressaillit, puis se mit à bégayer: 'Un service, Monsieur, rien qu'un petit service. Excusez-moi.' Il sortit de sa poche une carte de visite, écrivit rapidement une adresse sur le revers, et me la donna. 'Au nom de tout ce qui vous est précieux' me dit-il, 'venez à cette adresse demain vers midi, présentez cette carte, dites que vous êtes le Toulousain, dites que. . . .' Je lui coupai la parole. 'Monsieur' lui dis-je, 'je n'en ferai rien et je ne viendrai pas. Je ne vous connais pas, vous m'avez

insulté, vous. . . .' 'Mais si' insista-t-il, presque avec impatience, 'mais si, vous viendrez.' Puis, insolemment: 'Seriez-vous si bête . . . .' Il se tut. Enfin, et doucement cette fois: 'Mais pas avant midi', et là-dessus il sortit.

J'ai fait tout ce qu'il m'avait demandé. Il avait laissé chez la concierge un gros paquet adressé à 'mon cher ami de Toulouse qui a promis de venir.' 'Qui est ce Monsieur?' demandai-je à la concierge. Elle ne répondit pas. 'Qui est cet idiot? Où est-il?' J'étais furieux. 'Paraît qu'il est mort' me dit-elle.

Et voilà, Monsieur, tout ce que j'en sais, et je vous garantis que cela me suffit largement. Dans le paquet il n'y avait que les cahiers qui vous ont si fort intrigué. Je les ai transmis au conservateur de notre bibliothèque, d'abord pour m'en débarasser au plus vite et ensuite dans l'espoir que, perdus entre toutes les pourritures de cette maison des morts et des moribonds, ils ne sauront plus troubler personne. Il ne me reste que d'exprimer tous mes regrets que cette noble aspiration ne se soit pas réalisée, et de vous prier, Monsieur, d'agréêr ma sympathie et mon plus profond mépris.

Signé:

Il n'y a pas que les coups d'encensoir échangés avec une si triste patience entre le voleur et le frôleur de gloire qui soient inédits. Je déplore l'absence de son Altesse Sérénissime de Monaco. Car je suis vraiment le premier à violer ce sujet, et je sais avec quelle violence les coeurs nobles sont activés par une matière intacte, même si elle ne dispose pas des pièces de conviction d'une amitié miraculeuse. Intacte et parfaitement obscure. Pas de scandale, pas de sensation. Des concierges, beaucoup de concierges. Jean du Chas souffrait d'une véritable obsession à cet égard et il en avait une conscience très nette. 'Le concierge' a-t-il écrit dans un de ses cahiers, 'est la pierre angulaire de mon édifice entier.' Mais il nous présente un concierge pour ainsi dire idéal, idéal et abstrait, un concierge absolu, qui ne sait potiner. De nombreuses indications textuelles m'inclinent à voir dans ce motif presque névralgique le symbôle d'une de ces terribles manifestations de la nature, terribles et irrégulières, qui déchirent l'harmonie cosmique et démentissent tous ceux pour qui l'artisan de la création est le prototype de l'artiste néo-classique et l'enchaînement précaire des mois et des saisons un manifeste rassurant et cathartique: par exemple, une de ces averses ex nihilo qui ponctuent, heureusement à des intervalles assez espacés, le climat de cette île. Mais ce n'est là qu'une spéculation et si j'en ai parlé dès le début de mon discours c'est afin que vous preniez connaissance au plus tôt de la qualité sobre, unie, je dirai presque monochrome, de l'art chasien.

Jean du Chas, fils unique, illégitime et posthume d'un agent de change belge, mort en 1906 par suite d'une maladie de peau, et de Marie Pichon, vendeuse dans une maison de couture à Toulouse, et né à l'ombre rouge de la Basilique St Sernin, un peu avant midi le 13 avril 1906, aux divagations feutrées d'un carillon en deuil. A part les circonstances peu édifiantes de sa mort, nous ne savons rien de son père. Sa mère était d'origine allemande et entretenait des rapports suivis avec sa grand'mère, Annalisa Brandau, qui dirigeait toute seule, et, paraît-il, avec une habileté surhumaine, sa petite propriété aux bords de la Fulda, tout près de Kragenhof, ancienne station de villégiature et qui n'est plus maintenant qu'un vague éboulis de toits asphyxiés sous la houle des sapins. Dès l'âge de quatre ans il y allait tous les étés avec sa mère, et il évoque, dans un de ses premiers poèmes, la lente usure de toute sa sève de jeune Toulousain dans cette Tolomée de colophane. C'est à ces juvéniles expériences de fièvre allemande qu'il attribue l'impossibilité où il s'est trouvé pendant toute sa vie de dissocier l'idée de lumière de celles de chaleur et de dégoût. Pour lui il n'y a pas de spectacle plus exaspérant qu'un coucher de soleil — 'infecte déflagration' écrit-il, 'qui implique dans ses vomissements de paysagiste intoxiqué l'éternelle lassitude de Vesper', et il rejette cette vulgarité de carte postale en faveur de crépuscule plombé qui sert de fond blafard à la plus radieuse pâleur de Vénus. Et il salue le subtil désaccord si souvent et si vainement poursuivi d'un caillou à peine visible contre un front exsangue.

Négligé par sa mère, sans amis, maladif et sujet dès son plus jeune âge à ce qu'il a appelé des 'crises de négation', il traverse tant bien que mal une jeunesse qu'il n'aura ni le temps ni l'occasion de regretter. Le 13 avril, 1927, il écrit dans son journal: 'Me voici majeur, et malgré moi et malgré tout', et plus loin: 'Ces miracles immotivés ne sont point à mon goût'. Les notes de ce jour-là s'achèvent sur une phrase biffée avec une telle violence que le papier en a été déchiré. J'ai réussi à en reconstituer la seconde moitié. La voici: 'et il faut battre sa mère pendant qu'elle est jeune'. Son journal abonde en ces étranges interpolations. Il s'interrompt au milieu de détails triviaux et intimes pour écrire, entre parenthèses et en lettres majuscules: 'les éléphants sont contagieux'. Une autre fois c'est: 'je suis venu, je me suis assis, je suis parti' ou 'les curés ont toujours peur' ou 'user sa corde en se pendant' ou 'ne jeter aux démons que les anges'. Jean du Chas est mort à Marseille le 15 janvier 1928, dans un petit hôtel. L'avant-veille il avait écrit dans son Journal: 'mourir quand il n'est plus temps'. La page suivante, celle du 14, ne fournit que des objurgations à l'intention de Marseille et des Marseillais, et des projets de voyage. 'Cette cité est vraiment trop comique et la faune trop abondante et trop déclamatoire, sans intérêt. Folchetto est mort garçon. Moi aussi. Tant pis. J'irai m'embêter ailleurs. J'irai me confesser à Ancone'.

C'est bien la formule de son inquiétude, la constellation de tous ses déplacements: *va t'embêter ailleurs*, le stimulus qui finit par s'user à force de surmenage. Cette vie, telle qu'elle se dégage, vide et fragmentaire, de l'unique source disponible, son Journal, est une de ces vies horizontales, sans sommet, toute en longueur, un phénomène de mouvement, sans possibilité d'accélération ni de ralentissement, déclenché, sans être inauguré, par l'accident d'une naissance, terminé, sans être conclu, par l'accident d'une mort. Et vide, creuse, sans contenu, abstraction faites des vulgarités machinales de l'épiderme, celles qui s'accomplissent sans que l'âme en prennent connaissance. De vie sociale, pas une trace. En lisant son Journal on a l'impression que pour cet homme et fatalement et en dehors de toute action d'orgueil ou de mépris, la vie sociale, la convention sociale, toute l'ennuyeuse et prudente stylisation des afflictions humaines, amour, amitié, gloire et le reste, que tout cela n'était qu'une dimension, ou l'attribut d'une dimension, inévitable, comme la friction, une condition de son adhésion à la surface de la terre. De sorte que du Chas avait une vie sociale comme vous avez une vie centripète, à savoir, inconsciemment et indifféremment, ce qui équivaut à dire qu'il en était exempt, car l'indifférence et l'inconscience ne cadrent guère avec la tradition sacrosainte de la cave et la peur et l'ignorance et la solidarité crispée sous le tonnerre. Excluant et exclu, il traverse l'élément social, sans le juger. On aurait beau lui demander un jugement général, une critique compréhensive de tendances locales et actuelles. 'La faune est trop abondante': voilà tout ce qu'il peut en savoir. Toujours la faune, le mystère, accepté comme tel, sans intérêt, à Marseille comme partout, sauf qu'elle y pèse trop, y est trop prolongée dans l'espace, il en est accablé, faut aller s'embêter ailleurs. Et c'est toujours ainsi qu'il en parle, en constatations effectives, sans enthousiasme et sans colère, avec regret, mais sans en vouloir à qui ou à quoi que ce soit, comme un homme qui dirait, avant de demander son vestiaire: 'j'ai mangé trop d'huîtres'.

Telle était sa vie, une vie d'individu, le premier individu européen depuis l'expédition d'Egypte. Les acrobaties impériales ont flétri l'âme léonardesque, empoisonné la tranquille vertu des indifférents européens. Sous l'égide crapuleuse d'un valet cornélien la dernière trace de la colère dantesque s'est transformée en crachats de Jésuite fatigué, le cortège des pestiférés buboniques qui vont empuantir le 19e siècle s'organise à la gloire éternelle du premier touriste. C'en est fait. Montaigne s'appelle Baedeker, et Dieu porte un gilet rouge. Des minorités se mobilisent et inventent un vampire abstrait qu'elles appellent la majorité. C'est l'apothéose de la force mineure. Une horde de crapauds sadiques parcourent l'Europe à la recherche de l'ânesse éternellement exténuée. Raskolnikoff, Rastignac et Sorel se dévouent et mettent la Trinité au goût du jour, triangle scalène ou symbôle phallique, comme vous voulez, camarades. Chacun à sa gouttière. Ibsen prouve qu'il a raison. Renan démontre qu'il a tort. Coïncidence. Anatole France s'en fout à tue-tête. Marcel Proust se métamorphose en aubépine à force de fumigations. Coïncidence. Et Gide se crucifie à un angle de 69 degrés parce qu'il a perdu la concordance du chasseur et Fargue s'horizontalise parce qu'il a épuisé son répertoire de saloperies et Valéry décompose en propositions absolues ce qu'il n'a pas lu et Mallarmé bémolise en tierces clair-de-lunaires ce qu'il n'a pas fait et tous les autres que vous savez accordent leurs cornemuses et puis se mettent en quatre afin de jouer faux, car, saperlipopette!, les individus ne vont pas au concert. Enfin, et pour en finir de cette crise de splénite, si j'ose vous affirmer qu'un individu — (et je vous invite à verser dans ce mot, creux depuis un siècle, toute sa vertu prénapoléonique) — qu'un tel individu a vécu et est mort au milieu de nos vulgarités, c'est parce que je le trouve pur de cette exaspération sociale qui s'est nécessairement exprimée en braiements anti-sociaux, infiniment moins émouvants et moins nobles que les plus ordinaires explosions de tristesse asine. Et cela fait déjà deux fois, au cours de cette comédie, et dans l'espoir d'éclairer mon texte, que j'ai insulté l'âne. Je lui demande pardon. Je me prosterne devant ce plus charmant et plus ténébreux de tous les animaux qui nous font patiemment l'honneur d'agréer nos accès de tendresse. Mais le dernier affront, celui d'Esope, celui pour lequel il n'y a pas de rémission, et qui consiste à le faire parler, lui, l'âne, Dieu m'est témoin que je n'en suis pas encore coupable.

Vous allez trouver que la rubrique sociale a été soumise à une torsion de coup un peu prolongée. Et c'est bien le cas de dire: faute de mieux. Car il n'y a que cela. Tout est là-dedans. Si vous avez compris pourquoi du Chas est individu tandis que Gide ne l'est pas et ne le sera jamais, vos malheurs sont presque terminés. La chose s'explique. Et la membrane chasienne cède devant vos paroxysmes de pression cérébrale. Dispersion du concentrisme.

Je n'ai trouvé qu'un seul passage dans les Cahiers qui puisse, en dépit de sa façade rebarbative, nous éclairer à ce sujet. La voici intégralement:

'Mes enfants, mes tendres thyrsifères, lâchez la mamelle, faites attention à ce que je vais vous dire. Je sais que dans 10 ans vous ne demanderez pas mieux que de faire plaisir à mes mânes. Or, mes mânes seront difficiles. Du moins, j'ai lieu de le croire. Une de ces dévotions bruyantes et sanguines, semblables à celle que feu Monsieur mon père a vouée au sel de mercure, ne vous avancera en rien. Je ne veux, mes enfants, ni de vos approbations de scala santa ni de vos immortalités de basse-cour. Et c'est afin de m'en mettre à l'abri que je vous expose, ici et maintenant, votre programme. Vous allez vous appeler les *Concentristes*. C'est moi qui vous le dis, moi, inventeur du Concentrisme, moi, le Bouddha biconvexe. Vous direz à vos contemporains: — Jean du Chas, illustre fondateur de notre ordre, inventeur du Concentrisme, le Bouddha biconvexe, fils unique, illégitime et posthume d'un agent de change belge et d'une salaudine germano-toulousaine, vous invite, tutti quanti, à un festin religio-géologique, où vous pourrez vous farcir, à perte de boutons, de sainte nourriture sous la double forme de lentilles cartesiennes et concierges synthétiques. — Vous leur accorderez une courte pause et puis vous leur direz: — La poésie chasienne, c'est l'étirement d'une phrase dont les pétales s'ouvrent, *cordon s'il vous plaît* qui se désagrège sous les sourcillades de notre indomptable capitaine, qui, hélas!, lui aussi, a connu sa Suède. C'est en lui que nous saluons — et nous vous faisons l'honneur de vous inviter à en faire autant — l'auteur du *Discours de la Sortie*, conçu et composé parmi les chaudes vapeurs de la conciergerie, de toutes les concierges, poêles de Neuburg novecenteschi. — Et vous finirez par leur flanquer la définition suivante: — *Le Concentrisme est un prisme sur l'escalier*. Et voilà, mes enfants, les côtes de votre manifeste. Engraissez-le. Adieu, mes enfants, et bon appétit. Je vous rends à vos mères.'

Il ne faut pas se laisser bafouer par l'amère superficie de ce passage. Il ne faut pas non plus lui en vouloir d'une obscurité qui a l'air féroce en sa préméditation. Du Chas est ainsi. C'est un de ces esprits qui ne peuvent s'expliquer. Rien que l'idée d'une apologie, de la réduction de sa substance en hoquets universitaires — ce qu'il appelle: *reductio ad obscenum* — lui crispe et enchevêtre les nerfs. Ce n'est pas ainsi qu'il veut être compris. Ce n'est pas ainsi qu'il comprend la compréhension. Ses Cahiers contiennent plusieurs notes qui ne laissent pas de doute à cet égard. J'en choisis le plus clair et le plus susceptible de vous intéresser en vertu de son actualité:

'Je viens de lire une lettre de Proust' écrit-il, 'à l'intention de je ne sais plus qui, une (ou devrais-je dire: un) de ses Albertines-Jupiens sans doute, et où il explique pour quelles raisons il ne peut pas, mais absolument pas, se moucher le dimanche matin avant six heures. Le microcosme de sa thèse, ayant dégringolé par toute la hauteur d'une pagode invertie de tergiversations téléologiques, débouche en bolide victorieuse et vous broie la sensibilité'. Voici la dernière phrase de cette lettre: — 'de sorte que je me vois condamné, par suite de ce funeste enchaînement de circonstances qui remonte, n'en doutez pas, à quelque coryza mérovingien refoulé, pareil à Françoise qui, en ce moment même, blottie et invisible contre la caisse sonore de ma porte, se penche sur l'abîme fatal et délicieux d'un éternuement titanique, à aspirer les torrents de lave muceuse qui se soulèvent des profondeurs de ma morve matinale, sabbataire et volcanique et assiègent les soupapes frissonantes de mes narines. —'

Je n'ai jamais pu trouver cette lettre. Du Chas l'a peut-être fabriquée de toutes pièces. Elle est assez 'à la manière de . . .' pour être apocryphale. Mais cela n'a aucune espèce d'importance. Ce sont les réactions chasiennes qui nous concernent. Il précise la nature de son dégoût:

'Qu'il ne puisse se moucher le dimanche matin avant six heures, c'est une chose qui me semble assez naturelle. Mais après ce supplice de clarifications je n'y comprends plus rien. Au diable avec ses explications! Il n'y a que les tics justifiés qui soient indécents. La folie, Dieu merci, est indivisible.'

On pourrait tirer une variété de conclusions du manifeste des Concentristes tel que du Chas l'a ébauché dans son Journal. C'est une de ces énonciations qui se laissent volontiers réduire en assez d'obscénités pour satisfaire l'aspiration de chacun de nous vers les régions d'ordre et de clarté. Vous pourriez, par exemple, interpréter ce Discours de la Sortie comme l'expression artistique des évasions qui précèdent le suicide, et 'cordon s'il vous plaît' comme l'unique acte définitif de l'individu qui se fait enfin plus que justice. Ce serait un 'cogito ergo sum' un peu sensationnel. Et le concierge, celui qui laisse sortir? Tout ce que vous voudrez, Dieu ou la fatigue, petite attaque ou clairvoyance racinienne. Décomposition des joyeux qui descendent en colimaçon. Et vous voilà. Clair et conséquent comme les syllogismes de Monsieur Chauvin. Ou vous pourriez considérer tout cela sous la lumière de la physiologie. Ce serait plus égayant. Mais ce qui est certain, c'est que, si vous insistez à solidifier l'Idée, Celle dont il parle, à concréter la Chose de Kant, vous ne ferez que dégrader en vaudeville de Labiche cet art qui, semblable à une résolution de Mozart, est parfaitement intelligible et parfaitement inexplicable.

4. Dream of Fair to Middling Women

a. Supposing we told now a little story about China in order to orchestrate when we mean. Yes? Lîng-Liûn then, let us say, went to the confines of the West, to Bamboo Valley, and having cut there a stem between two knots and blown into same, was charmed to constate that it gave forth the sound of his own voice when he spoke, as he mostly did, without passion. From this the phoenix male had the kindness to sing six notes and the phoenix female six other notes and Lîng-Liûn the minister cut yet eleven stems to correspond with all that he had heard. Then he remitted the twelve liŭ-liū to his master, the six liŭ male phoenix and the six liū female phoenix: the Yellow Bell, let us say, the great Liū, the great Steepleiron, the Stifled Bell, the Ancient Purification, the Young Liū, the Beneficient Fecundity, the Bell of the Woods, the Equable Rule, the Southern Liū, the Imperfect, the Echo Bell.

Now the point is that it is most devoutly to be hoped that some at least of our characters can be cast for parts in a liŭ-liū. For example, John might be the Yellow Bell and the Smeraldina-Rima the Young Liū and the Syra-Cusa the Stifled Bell and the Mandarin the Ancient Purification and Belacqua himself the Beneficient Fecundity or the Imperfect, and so on. Then it would only be a question of juggling like Confucius on cubes of jade and playing a tune. If all our characters were like that — liŭ-liū-minded — we could write a little book that would be purely melodic; think how nice that would be, linear, a lovely Pythagorean chain-chant solo of cause and effect, a one-fingered teleophony that would be a pleasure to hear (which is more or less, if we may say so, what one gets from one's favourite novelist). But what can you do with a person like Nemo who will not for any consideration be condensed into a liū, who is not a note at all but the most regrettable simultaneity of notes. Were it possible to oralize say half-a-dozen Lîng-Liûn phoenices arising as one immortal purple bird from the ashes of a common pyre and crying simultaneously,

43

as each one saw fit, a cry of satisfaction or of disappointment, a rough idea of the status of this Nemo might be obtained: a symphonic, not a melodic, unit. Our line bulges every time he appears. Now that is a thing that we do not like to happen, and the less so as we are rather keenly aware of the infrequency of one without two. Dare we count on the Alba? Dare we count on Chas? Indeed we tend, on second thoughts, to smell the symphonic rat in our principal boy. He might just manage, semel et simul, the Beneficent Fecundity and the Imperfect; or, better still, furnish a bisexual bulge with a Great Iron of the woods. But ping! a mere liŭ! We take leave to doubt it. . . .

The real presence was a pest because it did not give the imagination a break. Without going as far as Stendhal, who said — or repeated after somebody — that the best music (What did he know about music anyway?) was the music that became inaudible after a few bars, we do declare and mantain stiffly (at least for the purposes of this paragraph) that the object that becomes invisible before your eyes is, so to speak, the brightest and best.

b. The night firmament is abstract density of music, symphony without end, illumination without end, yet emptier, more sparsely lit, than the most succinct constellations of genius. Now seen merely, a depthless lining of hemisphere, its crazy stippling of stars, it is the passional movements of the mind charted in light and darkness. The tense passional intelligence, when arithmetic abates, tunnels, skymole, surely and blindly (if we only thought so!) through the interstellar coalsacks of its firmament in genesis, it twists through the stars of its creation in a network of loci that shall never be co-ordinate. The inviolable criterion of poetry and music, the non-principle of their punctuation is figured in the demented perforation of the night colander. The ecstatic mind, the mind achieving creation, take ours for example, rises to the shaft-heads of its statement, its recondite relations of emergal, from a labour and a weariness of deep castings that brook no schema. The mind suddenly entombed, then active in an anger and a rhapsody of energy, in a scurrying and plunging towards exitus, such is the ultimate mode and factor of the creative integrity, its proton, incommunicable; but there, insistent, invisible rat, fidgeting behind the astral incoherence of the art surface. That was the circular movement of the mind flowering up and up through darkness to an apex, dear to Dionysius the Aeropagite, beside which all other modes, all the polite obliquities, are the clockwork of rond-de-cuirdom.

c. Pride of place to our boys and girls. Ah these liŭs and liūs! How have they stayed the course? Have they been doing their dope? The family, the Alba, the Polar Bear, Chas, that dear friend, and of course Nemo, ranging always from his bridge, seem almost as good as new, so little have they been plucked and blown and bowed, so little struck with the little hammer. But they will let us down, they will insist on being themselves, as soon as they are called for a little strenuous collaboration. Ping! they will no doubt cry with a sneer, pure, permanent lius, we? We take leave to doubt that. And far be it from us to condemn them on that account. But observe what happens in that event, we mean of our being unable to keep those boys and girls up to their notes. The peak pierces the clouds like a sudden flower. We call the whole performance off, we call the book off, it tails off in a horrid manner. The whole fabric comes unstitched, it goes ungebund, the wistful fabric. The music comes to pieces. The notes fly about all over the place, a cyclone of electrons. And then all we can do, if we are not too old and tired by that time to be interested in making the best of a bad job, is to deploy a curtain of silence as rapidly as possible.

At the same time we are bound to admit, placing ourselves for the moment in the thick of the popular belief that there are two sides to every question, that the territorials may behave, at least to the extent of giving us some kind of a meagre codetta. May they. There is many a slip, we all know that, between pontem and fontem and gladium and jugulum. But what that consideration has to do with our counting on members of the Dublin contingent to perform like decent indivisibilities is not clear. The fact of the matter is, we do not trust them. And why not? Because, firstly, of what has gone before; and, secondly, and here is the real hic, the taproot of the whole tangle, of our principal boy's precarious ipsissimosity.

Consequently, we are rather anxious to dilate briefly of these two things: one, the lius that have let us down; two, Belacqua, who can scarcely fail to keep on doing so.

d. Such a paraphrased abrégé would seem to indicate, unless there be some very serious flaw in our delirium, that the book is degenerating into a kind of Commedia dell'Arte, a form of literary statement to which we object particularly. The lius do just what they please, they just please themselves. They flower out and around into every kind of illicit ultra and infra and supra. Which is bad, because as long as they do that, they can never meet. We are afraid to call for the simplest chord. Belacqua drifts about, it is true, doing his best to thicken the tune, but harmonic composition properly speaking, music in depth on the considerable scale is, and this is a terrible thing to have to say, ausgeschlossen.

e. Much of what has been written concerning the reluctance of our refractory constituents to bind together is true equally of Belacqua. Their movement is based on a principle of repulsion, their property not to combine but, like heavenly bodies, to scatter and stampede, astral straws on a time-strom, grit in the mistral. And not only to shrink from all that is not they, from all that is without and that in its turn shrinks from them, but also to strain away from themselves. They are no good from the builder's point of view, firstly because they will not suffer their systems to be absorbed in the cluster of a greater system, and then, and chiefly, because they themselves tend to disappear as systems. Their centres are wasting, the strain away from the centre is not to be gainsaid, a little more and they explode. Then, to complicate things further, they have odd periods of recueillement, a kind of centripetal backwash that checks the rot. The procédé that seems all falsity, that of Balzac, for example, and the divine Jane and many others, consists in dealing with the vicissitudes, or absence of vicissitudes, of character in this backwash, as though that were the whole story. Whereas, in reality, this is so little the story, this nervous recoil into composure, this has so little to do with the story, that one must be excessively concerned with a total precision to allude to it at all. To the item thus artificially immobilized in a backwash of composure precise value can be assigned. So all the novelist has to do is to bind his material in a spell, item after item, and juggle politely with irrefragable values, values that can assimilate other values like in kind and be assimilated by them, that can increase and decrease in virtue of an unreal permanence of quality. To read Balzac is to receive the impression of a chloroformed world. He is absolute master of his material, he can do what he likes with it, he can foresee and calculate its least vicissitude, he can write the end of his book before he has finished the first paragraph, because he has turned all his creatures into clockwork cabbages and can rely on their staying put wherever needed or staying going at whatever speed in whatever direction he chooses. The whole thing, from beginning to end, takes place in a spellbound backwash. We all love and lick up Balzac, we lap it up and say it is wonderful, but why call a distillation of Euclid and Perrault *Scenes from Life*? Why *human* comedy?

f. 'Black diamond of pessimism.' Belacqua thought that was a nice example, in the domain of words, of the little sparkle hid in ashes, the precious margaret and hit from many, and the thing that the conversationalist, with his contempt of the tag and the ready-made, can't give you, because the lift to the high spot is precisely from the tag and the ready-made. The same with the stylist. You couldn't experience a margarita in d'Annunzio because he denies you the pebbles and flints that reveal it. The uniform, horizontal writing, flowing without accidence, of the man with a style, never gives you the margarita. But the writing of, say, Racine or Malherbe, perpendicular, diamanté, is pitted, is it not, and sprigged with sparkles; the flints and pebbles are there, no end of humble tags and commonplaces. They have no style, they write without style, do they not, they give you the phrase, the sparkle, the precious margaret. Perhaps only the French can do it. Perhaps only the French language can give you the thing you want.

Don't be too hard on him, he was studying to be a professor.

g. 'Get thee to a stud,' said Belacqua.

'Your vocabulary of abuse,' said the Mandarin, 'is arbitrary and literary, and at times comes close to entertaining me. But it doesn't touch me. You cannot touch me. You simplify and dramatize the whole thing with your literary mathematics. I don't waste any words with the argument of experience, the inward decrystallization of experience, because your type never accepts experience, nor the notion of experience. So I speak merely from a need that is as valid as yours, because it is valid. The need to live, to be authentically and seriously and totally involved in the life of my heart and . . .'.

'Have you forgotten the English for it?' said Belacqua.

'My heart and my blood. The reality of the individual, you had the cheek to inform me once, is an incoherent reality and must be expressed incoherently. And now you demand a stable architecture of sentiment.'

The Mandarin shrugged his shoulders. There was no shrug in the world, and not many shoulders, like the Mandarin's.

'You misunderstand me,' said Belacqua. 'What you heard me say does not concern my contempt for your dirty erotic manoeuvres. I was speaking of something of which you have and can have no knowledge, the incoherent continuum as expressed by, say, Rimbaud and Beethoven. Their names occur to me. The terms of whose statements serve merely to delimit the reality of the insane areas of silence, whose audibilities are no more than punctuation in a statement of silences. How do they get from point to point. That is what I meant by the incoherent reality and its authentic extrinsecation.'

'How,' said the Mandarin patiently, 'do I misunderstand you?'

'There is no such thing,' said Belacqua wildly, 'as a simultaneity of incoherence, there is no such thing as love in a thalamus. There is no word for such a thing, there is no such abominable thing. The notion of an unqualified present — the mere "I am" — is an ideal notion. That of an incoherent present — "I am this and that" — altogether abominable. I admit Beatrice,' he said kindly, 'and the brothel, Beatrice after the brothel or the brothel after Beatrice, but not Beatrice in the brothel, or rather, not Beatrice and me in bed in the brothel. Do you get that,' cried Belacqua, 'you old dirt, do you? not Beatrice and me in bed in the brothel!'

h. 'I shall write a book,' [Belacqua] mused, tired of the harlots of earth and air. 'I am hemmed in,' he submused, 'on all sides by putes, in thought or in deed, hemmed in and about; a giant big man must be hired to lift the hem — a book where the phrase is self-consciously smart and slick, but of a smartness and slickness other than that of its neighbours on the page. The blown roses of a phrase shall catapult the reader into the tulips of the phrase that follows. The experience of my reader shall be between the phrases, in the silence, communicated by the intervals, not the terms, of the statement, between the flowers that cannot coexist, the antithetical' (nothing so simple as antithetical) 'seasons of words, his experience shall be the menace, the miracle, the memory, of an unspeakable trajectory.' (Thoroughly worked up by now by this programme, he pushed himself off the bulwark and strode the spit of the deck with long strides and rapidly.) 'I shall state silences more competently than ever a better man spangled the butterflies of vertigo. I think now . . . of the dehiscing, the dynamic décousu of a Rembrandt, the implication lurking behind the pictorial pretext threatening to invade pigment and oscuro; I think of the Selbstbildnis, in the toque and the golden chain, of his portrait of his brother, of the cute little Saint Matthew angel that I swear van Ryn never saw the day he painted, in all of which canvases during lunch on many a Sunday I have discerned a disfaction, a désuni, an Ungebund, a flottement, a tremblement, a tremor, a tremolo, a disaggregating, a disintegrating, an efflorescence, a breaking down and multiplication of tissue, the corrosive ground-swell of Art. It is the Pauline *cupio dissolvi*. It is Horace's *solvitur acris hiems*. It might even be at a pinch poor Hölderlin's *alles hineingeht Schlangen gleich*. Schlangen gleich! . . . I think of Beethoven, his eyes are closed, the poor man he was very short-sighted they say, his eyes are closed, he smokes a long pipe, he listens to the ferns, the unsterbliche Geliebte, he unbuttons himself to Teresa ante rem, I think of his earlier compositions where into the body of the musical statement he incorporates a punctuation of dehiscence, flottements, the coherence gone to pieces, the continuity bitched to hell because the units of continuity have abdicated their unity, they have gone multiple, they fall apart, the notes fly about, a blizzard of electrons; and then the vespertine compositions eaten away with terrible silences, a music one and indivisible only at the cost of as bloody a labour as any known to man' (and woman? from the French horn) 'and pitted with dire stroms of silence, in which has been engulfed the hysteria that he used to let speak up, pipe up, for itself. And I think of the ultimately unprevisible atom threatening to come asunder, the left wing of the atom plotting without ceasing to spit in the eye of the physical statistician and commit a most copious offence of nuisance on his cenotaphs of indivisibility.

'All that,' conceded Belacqua, postponing the mare's-nest and the stars to another occasion, 'is a bit up in the rigging. If ever I do drop a book, which God forbid, trade being what it is, it will be ramshackle, tumbledown, a bone-shaker, held together with bits of twine, and at the same time as innocent of the slightest velleity of coming unstuck as Mr Wright's original flying-machine that could never be persuaded to leave the ground.'

But there he was probably wrong.

4. German Letter of 1937

9/7/37 6 Clare Street
Dublin
IFS

Lieber Axel Kaun!

Besten Dank für Ihren Brief. Ich war gerade im Begriff, Ihnen zu schreiben, als er kam. Dann habe ich verreisen müssen, wie Ringelnatz' männlicher Briefmark, obgleich unter weniger leidenschaftlichen Umständen.

Das Beste ist, ich sage Ihnen sofort und ohne Umschweife, Ringelnatz ist meiner Ansicht nach nicht der Mühe wert. Sie werden sicherlich nicht mehr enttäuscht sein, dies von mir zu hören, als ich es gewesen bin es feststellen zu müssen.

Ich habe die 3 Bände durchgelesen, 23 Gedichte ausgewählt und 2 von diesen als Probestücke übersetzt. Das wenige, was sie notwendigerweise dabei verloren haben, ist natürlich nur im Verhältnis mit dem zu schätzen, was sie eigentlich zu verlieren haben, und ich muss sagen, dass ich diesen Verschlechterungskoeffizienten, auch da, wo er am meisten Dichter ist, und am wenigsten Reimkuli, ganz gering gefunden habe.

Daraus ist gar nicht zu schliessen, dass ein übersetzter Ringelnatz weder Interesse noch Erfolg beim englischen Publikum finden würde. In dieser Beziehung aber bin ich vollkommen unfähig, ein Urteil zu fällen, da mir die Reaktionen des kleinen wie des grossen Publikums immer rätselhafter werden, und, was noch schlimmer ist, von weniger Bedeutung. Denn ich komme vom naiven Gegensatz nicht los, zumindest was die Literatur betrifft, dass eine Sache sich lohnt oder sich nicht lohnt. Und wenn wir unbedingt Geld verdienen müssen, machen wir es anderswo.

Ich zweifle nicht, dass Ringelnatz als Mensch von ganz ausserordentlichem Interesse war. Als Dichter aber scheint er Goethes Meinung gewesen zu sein: *Lieber NICHTS zu schreiben, als nicht zu schreiben*. Dem Uebersetzer aber hätte der Geheimrat selbst vielleicht gegönnt, sich dieses hohen Kakoethes unwürdig zu fühlen.

Ich würde mich freuen, Ihnen meinen Abscheu vor der Verswut Ringelnatz' genauer zu erklären, wenn Sie Lust haben, ihn zu verstehen. Vorläufig aber will ich Sie schonen. Vielleicht mögen Sie die Leichenrede ebensowenig wie ich.

Gleicherweise könnte ich Ihnen eventuell die ausgewählten Gedichte anzeigen und die Probeübersetzungen schicken.

*   *   *

Es freut mich immer, einen Brief von Ihnen zu bekommen. Schreiben Sie also möglichst häufig und ausführlich. Wollen Sie unbedingt, dass ich Ihnen auf Englisch das gleiche tue? Werden Sie beim Lesen meiner deutschen Brief ebenso gelangweilt, wie ich beim Verfassen eines englischen? Es täte mir Leid, wenn Sie das Gefühl hätten, es handele sich etwa um einen Kontrakt, dem ich nicht nachkomme. Um Antwort wird gebeten.

Es wird mir tatsächlich immer schwieriger, ja sinnloser, ein offizielles Englisch zu schreiben. Und immer mehr wie ein Schleier kommt mir meine Sprache vor, den man zerreissen muss, um an die dahinterliegenden Dinge (oder das dahinterliegende Nichts) zu kommen. Grammatik und Stil. Mir scheinen sie ebenso hinfällig geworden zu sein wie ein Biedermeier Badeanzug oder die Unerschütterlichkeit eines Gentlemans. Eine Larve. Hoffentlich kommt die Zeit, sie ist ja Gott sei Dank in gewissen Kreisen schon da, wo die Sprache da am besten gebraucht wird, wo sie am tüchtigsten missbraucht wird. Da wir sie so mit einem Male nicht ausschalten können, wollen wir wenigstens nichts versäumen, was zu ihrem Verruf beitragen mag. Ein Loch nach dem andern in ihr zu bohren, bis das Dahinterkauernde, sei es etwas oder nichts, durchzusickern anfängt — ich kann mir für den heutigen Schriftsteller kein höheres Ziel vorstellen.

Oder soll die Literatur auf jenem alten faulen von Musik und Malerei längst verlassenen Wege allein hinterbleiben? Steckt etwas lähmend Heiliges in der Unnatur des Wortes, was zu den Elementen der anderen Künste nicht gehört? Gibt es irgendeinen Grund, warum jene fürchterlich willkürliche Materialität der Wortfläche nicht aufgelöst werden sollte, wie z.B. die von grossen schwarzen Pausen gefressene Tonfläche in der siebten Symphonie von Beethoven, so dass wir sie ganze Seiten durch nicht anders wahrnehmen können als etwa einen schwindelnden unergründliche Schlünde von Stillschweigen verknüpfenden Pfad von Lauten? Um Antwort wird gebeten.

Ich weiss, es gibt Leute, empfindsame und intelligente Leute, für die es an Stillschweigen gar nicht fehlt. Ich kann nicht umhin anzunehmen, dass sie schwerhörig sind. Denn im Walde der Symbole, die keine sind, schweigen die Vöglein der Deutung, die keine ist, nie.

Selbstverständlich muss man sich vorläufig mit Wenigem begnünen. Zuerst kann es nur darauf ankommen, irgendwie eine Methode zu erfinden, um diese höhnische Haltung dem Worte gegenüber wörtlich darzustellen. In dieser Dissonanz von Mitteln und Gebrauch wird man schon vielleicht ein Geflüster der Endmusik oder des Allem zu Grunde liegenden Schweigens spüren können.

Mit einem solchen Programm hat meiner Absicht nach die allerletzte Arbeit von Joyce gar nichts zu tun. Dort scheint es sich vielmehr um eine Apotheose des Wortes zu handeln. Es sei denn, Himmelfahrt und Höllensturz sind eins und dasselbe. Wie schön wäre es, glauben zu können, es sei in der Tat so. Wir wollen uns aber vorläufig auf die Absicht beschränken.

Vielleicht liegen die Logographen von Gertrude Stein dem näher was ich im Sinne habe. Das Sprachgewebe ist wenigstens porös geworden, wenn nur leider ganz zufälligerweise, und zwar als Folge eines etwa der Technik von Feininger ähnlichen Verfahrens. Die unglückliche Dame (lebt sie noch?) ist ja ohne Zweifel immer noch in ihr Vehikel verliebt, wenn freilich nur wie ein Mathematiker in seine Ziffern, für den die Lösung des Problems von ganz sekundärem Interesse ist, ja ihm als Tod der Ziffern direkt schrecklich vorkommen muss. Diese Methode mit der von Joyce in Zusammenhang zu bringen, wie es die Mode ist, kommt mir genau so sinnlos vor wie der mir noch nicht bekannte Versuch den Nominalismus (im Sinne der Scholastiker) mit dem Realismus zu vergleichen. Auf dem Wege nach dieser für mich sehr wünschenswerten Literatur des Unworts, kann freilich irgendeine Form der nominalistischen Ironie ein notwendiges Stadium sein. Es genügt aber nicht, wenn das Spiel etwas von seinem heiligen Ernst verliert. Aufhören soll es. Machen wir es also wie jener verrückte (?) Mathematiker, der auf jeder einzelnen Stufe des Kalküls ein neues Messprinzip anzuwenden pflegte. Eine Wörterstürmerei im Namen der Schönheit.

Inzwischen mache ich gar nichts. Nur von Zeit zu Zeit habe ich wie jetzt den Trost, mich so gegen eine fremde Sprache unwillkürlich vergehen zu dürfen, wie ich es mit Wissen und Willen gegen meine eigene machen möchte und — Deo juvante — werde.

Mit herzlichem Gruss

Ihr

Soll ich Ihnen die Ringelnatz-Bände zurückschicken?
Gibt es eine englische Uebersetzung von Trakl?

5. Les Deux Besoins

'Et le pharmacien . . . entonna:

"J'ai deux grands boeufs dans mon étable.
Deux grand boeufs blancs. . . ."

Sénécal lui mit la main sur la bouche, il n'aimait pas le désordre.'

(Gustave Flaubert. *L'Education Sentimentale.*)

Il n'y a sans doute que l'artiste qui puisse finir par voir (et, si l'on veut, par faire voir aux quelques-uns pour qui il existe) la monotone centralité de ce qu'un chacun veut, pense, fait et souffre, de ce qu'un chacun est. N'ayant cessé de s'y consacrer, même alors qu'il n'y voyait goutte, mais avant qu'il n'eût accepté de n'y voir goutte, il peut à la rigueur finir par s'en apercevoir.

Il se mouvait pourtant, le berceau de Galilée.

Ce foyer, autour duquel l'artiste peut prendre conscience de tourner, comme la monade — sauf erreur — autour d'elle-même, on ne peut évidemment en parler, pas plus que d'autres entités substantielles, sans en falsifier l'idée. C'est ce que chacun fera à sa façon. L'appeler le besoin, c'est une façon comme une autre.

Les autres, les innombrables béats et sains d'esprit, l'ignorent. Ils ont beau être fixés du même trait, ils prennent les lieux dans l'état où ils se trouvent, ils ne laissent rien monter chez eux qui puisse compromettre la solidité des planchers. C'est à l'exclusion de grand besoin, sur lui si j'ose dire, qu'ils vaquent aux petits. D'où cette vie toute en marge de son principe, cette vie faite de décisions, de satisfactions, de réponses, de menus besoins assassinés, cette vie de plante à la croisée, de choux pensant et même bien pensant, la seule vie possible pour ceux qui se voient dans la nécessité d'en mener une, c'est à dire la seule vie possible.

Besoin de quoi? Besoin d'avoir besoin.

Deux besoins, dont le produit fait l'art. Qu'on se garde bien d'y voir un primaire et un secondaire. Il y a des jours, surtout en Europe, où la route réflète mieux que le miroir. Préférer l'un des testicules à l'autre, ce serait aller sur les platebandes de la métaphysique. A moins d'être le démon de Maxwell.

Falsifions davantage.

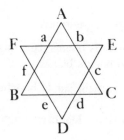

Besoin d'avoir besoin (DEF) et besoin dont on a besoin (ABC), conscience du besoin d'avoir besoin (ab) et conscience du besoin dont on a besoin — dont on *avait* besoin (de), issue du chaos de vouloir voir (Aab) et entrée dans le néant d'avoir vu (Dde), déclenchement et fin de l'autologie créatrice (abcdef). Voilà par exemple une façon comme une autre d'indiquer les limites entre lesquelles l'artiste se met à la question, se met en question, se résout en questions, en questions rhétoriques sans fonction oratoire.

Dodécahèdre régulier, trop régulier, suivant les dimensions duquel l'infortuné Tout-puissant se serait *proposé* d'arranger les quatre éléments, signature de Pythagore, divine figure dont la construction dépend d'un irrationnel, à savoir l'incommensurabilité de la diagonale de carré avec le côté, sujet sans nombre et sans personne. N'est-ce pas pour avoir trahi ce sombre secret que Hippasos a péri avant terme, lynché par la meute d'adeptes affamés, vierges et furibonds dans un égout public? Il n'était ni fasciste ni communiste.

Côté et diagonale, les deux besoins, les deux essences, l'être qui est besoin et la nécessité où il est de l'être, enfer d'irraison d'où s'élève le cri à blanc, la série de questions pures, l'oeuvre.

S'il est permis en pareil cas de parler d'un principe effectif, ce n'est pas, Dieu et Poincaré merci, celui qui régit les petitions de principe de la science et les logoi croisés de la théologie, qui alimente les tempêtes de pets affirmatifs et négatifs d'où sont sortis et sortent toujours ces foireux aposterioris de l'Esprit et de la Matière qui font le désespoir des peuples sauvages. Cela avance à coups de oui et de non comme un obus à détonateurs, jusqu'à ce que la vérité explose. Encore une. Irréversible. Les morts et les blessés en témoignent.

Autrement dit, le saint sorite, *lubricum et periculorum locus*. Rien ne ressemble moins au procès créateur que ces convulsions de vermisseau enragé, propulsé en spasmes de jugement vers une pourriture d'élection. Car aux enthymèmes de l'art ce sont les conclusions qui manquent et non pas les prémisses.

Jusqu'à nouvel avis.

Part II

Words About Writers

A. OTHER WRITERS

1. Schwabenstreich

Mozart On The Way To Prague. By Edward Moerike.

Here is a 'fragment of imaginative composition' short and not at all to the point, but at least short, which is nowadays so rare a quality in a literary work that one cannot refrain from commending this book for having contrived, in 20,000 words instead of in 200,000, to exhaust the inessential. Nevertheless, it is to be feared that some of those 'Mozart lovers' to whom it is dedicated may find the process overlong, as it undoubtedly was for Eduard Moerike, whose talent was sporadic, eager in attack and rapidly exhausted. That his was an energy intolerant of discursive amplification is plain to anyone who reads his *Balladen*, if possible more tedious than the *verkörpeter Mondschein* of his Minerva, Uhland; or the autobiographical *Maler Nolten*, which he frankly abandoned; or even the *Märchen* and *Novellen*. What he could do, when the fit seized him and he could snatch a moment from his professional engagements as pastor and pedagogue — for business never stood any nonsense from art in Swabia — to attend to the raptus, was write a lyric. *Denke' es, O Seele*, with which this story concludes, and *Ein Stündlein wohl vor Tag* are not inferior to anything in Eichendorff.

In the autumn of 1787 Mozart sets out from Vienna with his wife Kostanze to produce his *Don Giovanni* at Prague. They halt at midday; Mozart saunters into the pleasaunce of one Count Schinzberg, helps himself (with a pensive smile) to an orange, is apprehended by the gardener, dashes off his excuses to the Countess, proceeds on her invitation (Kappellmeister Mozart! Grande, grande Mozart!) to be installed with Kostanze in the Schloss and most comfortably and excellently entertained; sings, plays (billiards and Klavier), gorges, boozes, flirts, reminisces, performs in a free version some numbers of his *Don Giovanni*, from *Or sai, chi l'onore* no doubt to the 'trombones of silver' of the bloodcurdling Finale, sleeps the night, gratefully accepts in the morning the parting gift of a smart travelling carriage and proceeds on his way. Such is the material from which Herr Moerike has presumed to extract 'the picture of the artist's individuality'. What emerges is the species of paranoiac entertainer who, in the service of Archbishop Hieronymus, was greeted in such abusive terms as *Flegel*, *Lump* and *Gassenbube*.

Mozart's improvidence, his obsession with death, his creative processes (for which Moerike had the incredible impertinence to 'cherish a sense of affinity'), the theory of *Correspondances*, that trusty standby of all the Romantics from Hoffmann to Proust, these, together with certain inner obliquities embracing Madame de Sévigné and Mozart's saltbox, are the elements that complete the cartoon. There are a number of passages — the description of the orange exhaling its aria, the Neapolitan masque, the scene in a Viennese skittle-alley — that would be pleasant enough in a less pretentious context. But when such writing, valid as isolated exercises in lyrical prose, is pressed into an undertaking that has betrayed all the ingenuity and intelligence of men very much more highly endowed than Eduard Moerike, and in which all writing, *qua* writing, is bound to fail — the undertaking, that is, to elucidate the ultimate *Kunsttrieb* of a musical genius — then there is nothing at all to be said for it nor anything too strong to be said against it.

For it is not merely a betrayal of itself; it is a violation of its subject. No one is likely to question the right of Herr Moerike to make what abuse he pleased of his own peculiar talents, but he should have been restrained from presenting the *Hexenmeister* of the *Jupiter Symphony*, the *A Minor Sonata*, the *Requiem* and *The Magic Flute* as a compound of Horace Skimpole and Wagner in half-hose.

2. Proust in Pieces

Comment Proust a composé son Roman. Par Albert Feuillerat

The original edition of *A la Recherche du Temps Perdu*, as undertaken by Grasset in 1913, was to consist of three volumes, *Du Côté de Chez Swann, Le Côté de Guermantes* and *Le Temps Retrouvé*, or about 1,500 pages. This edition, when the first volume only had appeared, was interrupted by the War. The current edition, completed by the N.R.F. in 1924, consists of sixteen volumes or about 4,000 pages. Professor Feuillerat, as he perused this final version, was sensible of grave dissonances and incompatibilities, clashing styles, internecine psychologies and deplorable solutions of continuity, such chaos in short as could only be explained by the inharmonious collaboration of the two Prousts, the pre-War and the post-War, corresponding to the two periods of gestation, 1905–1912 and 1912–1922. Setting the separating machine in motion he restored order, extorted the original from the final text, reconstituted in fact volumes 2 and 3 as, but for the War, they might have been expected to come from Grasset. Next, anxious to establish his demonstration on the firm basis of a document, he shrewdly suspected, sought and found the uncorrected galley-sheets of volume 2 as announced by Grasset. *'Il faut peut-être porter en soi l'âme d'un de ces chercheurs de documents . . . pour comprendre les sentiments qui m'agitaient. Un grand espoir s'ouvrait.'* Professor Feuillerat, as he compared those precious proofs with his independent reconstruction of volume 2, found himself amply confirmed. And now he could offer to the public, not only a dreadnought survey of the changes imposed by Proust on a large portion of his work, but also, deduced rigorously from that cast-iron collation, the first draught of the remainder, Grasset's volume 3. And this in fact is what Professor Feuillerat has done.

What was his purpose in doing this? The publication of a great mind in the throes? Not merely, but, *la révélation d'un Proust assez différent de celui qu'on a imaginé*, that was the real purpose.

The revealed Proust is no less than trine. Here we have the Proust of 1905–12, of the galley-sheets, the evocator, opaquely analytic, transcribing in highly imaged terms the data of spontaneous memory; here again the Proust of 1912–22, of the 2,500 pages annexed to the original text, the dialectician, selecting and schematizing his material, writing a language that is hard and abstract; and here finally, lamentable resultant of the above agents, the Proust that to the casual reader, victim of superstitions concerning creative integrity, appears incomprehensible, the Proust esteemed by Gide, Cocteau, Dr Curtius, Ortega y Gasset and others. It is only by keeping the early Proust, proceeds Professor Feuillerat in the expert tone of one meting out a canvas between del Mazo and Velasquez, so distinct from the Proust of the 'resipiscence' as to obviate the smudge of their conjunction, that one can hope to resolve the perturbations and dislocations of the text as it stands and estimate the master at his true value. If Proust had lived, he would have so altered the original writing as to remove all discord and dissension, a beautiful unity of tone and treatment would have, as it were, embalmed the whole, and Professor Feuillerat's book need never have been written.

Uniformity, homogeneity, cohesion, selection scavenging for verisimilitude (the stock-in-trade exactly of the naturalism that Proust abominated), these are the Professor's tastes, and they are distressed by the passage of intuition and intellection hand in hand, by Mme de Marsantes a saint and a snob in the one breath, by the narrator boy and man without transition, by the inconsequences of Swann, Odette, Saint-Loup, Gilberte, Mme de Villeparisis and even poor Jupien, but most of all by the stupefying antics of those two indeterminates, Charlus and Albertine. And out of their distress they cry for the sweet reasonableness of plane psychology à la Balzac, for the narrational trajectory that is more like a respectable parabola and less like the chart of an ague, and for Time, proclaiming its day of the month and the state of its weather, to elapse in an orderly manner. It is almost as though Proust should be reproached for having written a social *Voyage of the Beagle*.

Professor Feuillerat rides the antithesis to death. There is no shortage of critical analysis in the original text, nor of impressionism in the interpolations. That which is added is an intensification, not a disclaimer, of the initial conception and method. If there is *mésalliance*, as for the purists there must be, it was there from the start. And is it not precisely this conflict between intervention and quietism, only rarely to be resolved through the uncontrollable agency of unconscious memory, and its statement without the plausible frills that constitute the essence of Proust's originality? The book is the search, stated in the full complexity of all its clues and blind alleys, for that resolution, and not the *compte rendu* after the event, of a round trip. His material, pulverized by time, obliterated by habit, mutilated in the clockwork of memory, he communicates as he can, in dribs and drabs. These, no doubt, when finally by chance the resolution is consummated in the Hôtel de Guermantes and the comedy announced as shortly to be withdrawn, may be added up, like those of a life, and cooked to give unity. But such a creditable act of integration would not do for Professor Feuillerat who desires, nay requires, that the right answer, the classical answer, should be ostentatiously implicit in every step of the calculation.

3. Poems. By Rainer Maria Rilke.

Translated from the German by J.B. Leishmann.

Malte Laurids Brigge was a kind of deficient Edmond Teste, deficient in his commerce with Svevo's *Zeno* and Gide's *Lafcadio*, a Teste who had not 'tué la marionette', a Teste obliged to rise, for the purpose of breathing, at frequent intervals to the surface of his 'variation'. So one feels it to be with Rilke, always popping up for the gulp of disgust that will rehabilitate the *Ichgott*, recruit him for the privacies of that divinity — until the next time.

Hence the breathless petulance of so much of his verse (he cannot hold his emotion) and the overstatement of the solitude which he cannot make his element. In the first of the two poems entitled 'The Solitary' that appear in Mr Leishmann's selection, the one taken from the *Buch der Bilder*, to which Maeterlinck would seem to have given the *la*, the other from the *Neue Gedichte*, written while under the thumb of Rodin, he indulges his sense of incommensurability in the crassest of antitheses: 'I move among these human vegetables. . . . But my horizon's full of phantasy.' It is the protest of a child who cannot pause to learn, as Heine learned, the fantasy investing 'human vegetables' (which expression, incidentally, does rather less than justice to *den ewig Einheimischen* of the original) and so at least postpone the disillusion of horizons abounding in the same product, a disillusion duly registered in the *Neue Gedichte* version: 'No, my heart shall turn into a tower . . .'. The mystic heart, geared to the *blaue Blume*, petrified! This is the very language of apostasy after the *Stundenbuch*, where God is the tower and the heart whatever you please to call it:

> Ich kreise um Gott, um den uralten Turm,
> Und ich kreise jahrtausendelang;
> Und ich weiss noch nicht; ich bin ein Falke, ein Sturm,
> Oder ein grosser Gesang.

Such a turmoil of self-deception and naif discontent gains nothing in dignity from that prime article of the Rilkean faith, which provides for the interchangeability of Rilke and God:

> Mit meinem Reifen
> reift
> dein Reich.

There is no position here, no possibility of a position, no faculty for one. He changes his ground without ceasing, like Gide, though for different reasons; not in order to save his bacon (oh in the very highest sense), but because he cannot stay still. He has the fidgets, a disorder which may very well give rise, as it did with Rilke on occasion, to poetry of a high order. But why call the fidgets God, Ego, Orpheus and the rest? This is a childishness to which German writers seem specially prone. Klopstock suffered from the fidgets all his life long, and called them *Messias*.

The translation gets least in the way when it follows its text most closely, for instance in the poem beginning 'Again and again'. The numerous deviations are unwarrantable, that is to say, ineffective, as when 'Keine Vision von fremden Ländern' blossoms forth as 'No dream of surf on southern coast-lines glancing', 'Lieder' is promoted to 'blithe songs' and the competent hysteria of

> 'Männer und Frauen; Männer, Männer, Frauen
> Und Kinder. . . .

made presentable as

> Men, women, women, men in black and grays,
> And children with their bright diversity. . . .

4. Humanistic Quietism

Poems. By Thomas McGreevy.

All poetry, as discriminated from the various paradigms of prosody, is prayer. A poem is poetry and not Meistergesang, Vaudeville, Fragrant Minute, or any of the other collects for the day, in so far as the reader feels it to have been the only way out of the tongue-tied profanity. This canon has one great advantage, that it passes as poetry more than it rejects as mere metre, a great advantage indeed, now that Balnibarbism has triumphed. For prayer may be 'good' in Dante's sense on any note between and inclusive of the publican's whinge and the pharisee's taratantara. When the changes are made we have the great publican poems (*Vita Nuova*, *Astrophel and Stella*, *On the death of Laura*, etc.) and the great pharisee poems (Goethe's *Prometheus*, Carducci's *Satan*, and the best of our domestic low church imprecations), to say nothing of their accommodation in a single period such as Milton contrived at the opening of *Paradise Lost*. But it is with neither of these extremes that we have to do here.

To the mind that has raised itself to the grace of humility 'founded' — to quote from Mr McGreevy's *T. S. Eliot* — 'not on misanthropy but on hope', prayer is no more (no less) than an act of recognition. A nod, even a wink. The flag dipped in Ave, not hauled down in Miserere. This is the adult mode of prayer syntonic to Mr McGreevy, the unfailing salute to *his* significant from which the fire is struck and the poem kindled, and kindled to a radiance without counterpart in the work of contemporary poets writing in English, who tend to eschew as understatement anything and everything between brilliance and murk. The equable radiance of —

> But a moment, now, I suppose,
> For a moment I may suppose,
> Gleaming blue,

> Silver blue,
> Gold,
> Rose,
> And the light of the world.
>
> *(Gloria de Carlos V)*

and of —

> The end of love,
> Love's ultimate good,
> Is the end of love . . . and
> Light . . .
>
> *(Seventh Gift of the Holy Ghost)*.

Even the long Cab Poem, the darkest, as I believe it to be the least characteristic, in this small volume of shining and intensely personal verse, climbs to its Valhalla, in this blaze of prayer creating its object: —

> Brightness of brightness,
> Towering in the sky
> Over Dublin . . .

obliterating the squalid elements of civil war.

It is from this nucleus of endopsychic clarity, uttering itself in the prayer that is a spasm of awareness, and from no more casual source, that Mr McGreevy evolves his poems. This is the energy and integrity of *Giorgionismo*, self-absorption into light; of the rapt Giorgionesque elucidations of *Recessional* and *Nocturne*; and of the admirable *Nocturne of the Self-Evident Presence*: —

> I see alps, ice, stars and white starlight
> In a dry, high silence.

He has seen it before, he shall see it again. For the intelligent Amiel there is only one landscape.

To know so well what one values is, what one's value is, as not to neglect those occasions (they are few) on which it may be doubled, is not a common faculty; to retain in the acknowledgment of such enrichment the light, calm and finality that composed it is an extremely rare one. I do not know if the first of these can be acquired; I know that the second cannot.

5. Recent Irish Poetry

I propose, as rough principle of individuation in this essay, the degree in which the younger Irish poets evince awareness of the new thing that has happened, or the old thing that has happened again, namely the breakdown of the object, whether current, historical, mythical or spook. The thermolaters — and they pullulate in Ireland — adoring the stuff of song as incorruptible, uninjurable and unchangeable, never at a loss to know when they are in the Presence, would no doubt like this amended to breakdown of the subject. It comes to the same thing — rupture of the lines of communication.

The artist who is aware of this may state the space that intervenes between him and the world of objects; he may state it as no-man's-land, Hellespont or vacuum, according as he happens to be feeling resentful, nostalgic or merely depressed. A picture by Mr Jack Yeats, Mr Eliot's 'Waste Land', are notable statements of this kind. Or he may celebrate the cold comforts of apperception. He may even record his findings, if he is a man of great personal courage. Those who are not aware of the rupture, or in whom the velleity of becoming so was suppressed as a nuisance at its inception, will continue to purvey those articles which, in Ireland at least, had ceased to be valid even before the literary advisers to J. M. Synge found themselves prematurely obliged to look elsewhere for a creative hack. These are the antiquarians, delivering with the altitudinous complacency of the Victorian Gael the Ossianic goods.

Thus contemporary Irish poets may be divided into antiquarians and others, the former in the majority, the latter kindly noticed by Mr W. B. Yeats as 'the fish that lie gasping on the shore', suggesting that they might at least learn to expire with an air. This position, needless to say, is not peculiar to Ireland or anywhere else. The issue between the conventional and the actual never lapses, not even when the conventional and the actual are most congruent. But it is especially acute in Ireland, thanks to the technique of our leading twilighters.

The device common to the poets of the Revival and after, in the use of which even beyond the jewels of language they are at one, is that of flight from self-awareness, and as such might perhaps be described as a convenience. At the centre there is no theme. Why not? Because the centre is simply not that kind of girl, and no more about it. And without a theme there can be no poem, as witness the exclamation of Mr Yeats's 'fánatic heart': 'What, be a singer born and lack a theme!' ('The Winding Stair'). But the circumference is an iridescence of themes — Oisin, Cuchulain, Maeve, Tir-nanog, the Táin Bo Cuailgne, Yoga, the Crone of Beare — segment after segment of cut-and-dried sanctity and loveliness. There are the specialists, but no monopolies, each poet being left perfect liberty to make his selection. The poem of poems would embrace the sense of confinement, the getaway, the vicissitudes of the road, the wan bliss on the rim. But a large degree of freedom may enter into the montage of these components, and it is very often in virtue of this, when the tics of mere form are in abeyance, that attributions are to be made. Thus typically the first may be scarcely perceptible in Mr Colum and even less so in Mr Stephens, the second predominate in Mr Yeats, the third be acutely dilated by Miss Pamela Travers or the Rev. Monk Gibbon, and the fourth to all intents and purposes discarded by George Russell who, when thoroughly galvanized by the protracted apathies, rigidities and abstractions, enters his heart's desire with such precipitation as positively to protrude into the void.

What further interest can attach to such assumptions as those on which the convention has for so long taken its ease, namely, that the first condition of any poem is an accredited theme, and that in self-perception there is no theme, but at best sufficient *vis a tergo* to land the practitioner into the correct scenery, where the self is either most happily obliterated or else so improved and enlarged that it can be mistaken for part of the *décor*? None but the academic. And it is in this connection that our lately founded Academy may be said to meet a need and enjoy a function.

Mr W. B. Yeats, as he wove the best embroideries, so he is more alive than any of his contemporaries or scholars to the superannuation of these, and to the virtues of a verse that shall be nudist. 'There's more enterprise in going naked.' It eliminates swank — unless of course the song has something to swank about. His bequest in 'The Tower' of his pride and faith to the 'young upstanding men' has something almost second-best bed, as though he knew that they would be embarrassed to find an application for those dispositions. Yet when he speaks, in his preface to Senator Gogarty's 'Wild Apples', of the 'sense of hardship borne and chosen out of pride' as the ultimate theme of the Irish writer, it is as though he were to derive in direct descent the very latest prize canary from that fabulous bird, the mesozoic pelican, addicted, though childless, to self-eviscerations.

Mr James Stephens in 'Theme and Variation' (1930) and 'Strict Joy' (1931), remains in his annexe of the tradition, where the poet appears as beauty expert:

> Yea, wonder is that he has done,
> For all that is beneath the sun
> By magic he transfigures to
> A better sound, a finer view.

> — ('Theme and Variations')

Then follows the psychometricization of Plotinus, rather less of a success than that practised on Descartes by La Fontaine. When the theme, without which there can be no poem, is in itself presentable, then its transmission is a mere question of metrical adjustments; but when it is not, when it is a mournful or a miserable thing, then it must be smartened up:

> . . . Because all things transfer
> From what they seem to what they truly are
> When they are innocently brooded on —
> And so the poet makes grief beautiful.

> — ('Strict Joy')

'Reverie on a Rose' is a good sample of this process — and a gloss on its innocency.

Mr Austin Clarke, having declared himself, in his 'Cattle-drive in Connaught' (1925), a follower of 'that most famous juggler, Mannanaun', continues in 'The Pilgrimage' (1920) to display the 'trick of tongue or two' and to remove, by means of ingenious metrical operations, 'the clapper from the bell of rhyme.' The fully licensed stock-in-trade from Aisling to Red Branch Bundling, is his to command. Here the need for formal justifications, more acute in Mr Clarke than in Mr Higgins, serves to screen the deeper need that must not be avowed.

Though in his 'Island Blood' (1925), 'The Dark Breed' (1927) and 'Arable Holdings' (1933) Mr Higgins has accumulated a greater number of 'By Gods' than all the other antiquarians put together, though he is less of the 'glimmering fawn' than Mr Russell and less of the lilter and lisper than Mr Colum or Mr Stephens, yet he is still victim of the centrifugal daemon:

> Come away to this holy air . . .
> Come away to this simple lake
>   And learn at the voice of a bird
> To vie with their music and make
>   New worlds in a word.
>
> — ('Island Blood')

It is agreeable, if unreasonable, to connect this impulse, the entire Celtic drill of extraversion, with Mr Higgins's blackthorn stick, thus addressed:

> And here, as in green days you were the perch,
> You're now the prop of song . . .
>
> — ('Arable Holdings')

His verses have what Ledwidge's had, what all modern nature poetry excepting Wordsworth's has, a good smell of dung, most refreshing after all the attar of far off, most secret and inviolate rose. And surely it is a great pity that the discernment enabling Mr Higgins to see his native land as 'an Easter Island in the Western Sea' should be so intolerant of its own company. It is symptomatic that both Mr Clarke and Mr Higgins are now taking up prose.

In 'For Daws to Peck At' (1929) and 'Seventeen Sonnets' (1932), the Rev. Monk Gibbon follows his secret heart from the 'lack-luck lot'. He is the poet of children ('Chacun Son Goût'), and as such is bound to consider thought a microbe:

> And, though the tune's of little count
> And knowledge more than all to me,
> Who knows what music may have died

73

When that small seed fell silently?
— ('For Daws To Peck At')

The sonnets, with so many definite and indefinite articles excised, recall the succinctness of the Cambridge Experimenters.

These, to whom Mr Brian O'Higgins, An Philibin and Miss Large may conveniently be annexed, are the chief of the younger antiquarians.

Mr Thomas MacGreevy is best described as an independent, occupying a position intermediate between the above and the poor fish, in the sense that he neither excludes self-perception from his work nor postulates the object as inaccessible. But he knows how to wait for the thing to happen, how not to beg the fact of this 'bitch of a world' — inarticulate earth and inscrutable heaven:

> I labour in a barren place,
> Alone, self-conscious, frightened, blundering;
> Far away, stars wheeling in space,
> About my feet, earth voices whispering.
> — ('Poems, 1934')

And when it does happen and he sees, 'far as sensitive eyesight could see', whatever happens to be dispensed, *gile na gile* or empty hearths, it is the act and not the object of perception that matters. Mr MacGreevy is an existentialist in verse, the Titchener of the modern lyric. It is in virtue of this quality of inevitable unveiling that his poems may be called elucidations, the vision without the dip, and probably the most important contribution to post-War Irish poetry.

There is much in Mrs Blanaid Salkeld's 'Hello Eternity' (1933) that is personal and moving, when not rendered blue in the face by the sonnet form. What is badly needed at the present moment is some small Malherbe of free verse to sit on the sonnet and put it out of action for two hundred years at least. Perhaps Mr Pound . . .? Other Irish sonneteers are Mr Erik Dodds ('Thirty-two poems', 1929) and Mr Francis Macnamara ('Marionettes', 1909), but only in the leisure moments of a university professor and a student of social theory respectively. The influence of Rossetti is strong in Mr Macnamara. The Oxford Georgians have left their mark on Mr Dodds.

In 'Man Poem' (1919) Mr Percy Usher, best known as translator of Merriman's 'Midnight Court', deals with himself and the vacuum in a manner that abides no question. One would like to see this work, before it is improved out of existence, safely between the boards.

Mr Francis Stuart is of course best known as a novelist, but he writes verse. So does Mr R. N. D. Wilson. So does Mr Leslie Yodaiken when his politics let him. So I am sure do Mr Frank O'Connor and Mr Seán O'Faoláin — also best known as novelists of course. And I know that Mr Seán O'Casey does, having read a poem of his in *Time and Tide*.

In 'Primordia Caeca' (1927) Mr Lyle Donaghy undertook a regular *Saison en Enfer*:

> Enter again into the womb;
>> be saturate with night;
>> let the vain soul be satisfied,
> Descend into the dark cell;
>> look on the unnatured, undistinguished pulp;
>> peruse the incipient page.
> Retrace the way come blindly;
>> from centre and cause revisited,
>> draw the pure being up.

It is drawn up, but in the unfinished condition made manifest in his 'Flute Over the Valley' (1931), which contains however a fine poem about a steam-roller. Some years ago Mr Donaghy published an admirable 'objectless' poem — 'The Fort' — in the *Criterion*. Another volume, 'Into the Light', is announced as impending. May it be down into the light.

Mr Geoffrey Taylor, in his 'Withering of the Fig-leaf' and 'It Was Not Jones', performed a very diverting ballet away from the pundits. But I do not know that he has done anything since.

Mr Denis Devlin and Mr Brian Coffey are without question the most interesting of the youngest generation of Irish poets, but I do not propose to disoblige them by quoting from the volume of verse which they published jointly in 1930. Since then they have submitted themselves to the influences of those poets least concerned with evading the bankrupt relationship referred to at the opening of this essay — Corbière, Rimbaud, Laforgue, the *surréalistes* and Mr Eliot, perhaps also to those of Mr Pound —

with results that constitute already the nucleus of a living poetic in Ireland:

> Phrases twisted through other
> Reasons reasons disproofs
> Phrases lying low
> Proving invalid that reason
> With which I prove its truth
> Identity obscured
> Like the reflections of
> One mirror in another
> Reasons reasons disproofs.

It is no disparagement of Mr Devlin to observe that this is still too much by the grace of Eluard. What matters is that it does not proceed from the *Gossoons Wunderhorn* of that Irish Romantic Arnim-Brentano combination, Sir Samuel Ferguson and Standish O'Grady, and that it admits — stupendous innovation — the existence of the author. *Es wandelt niemand ungestraft unter Palmen* is peculiarly applicable to these islands, where pigeons meet with such encouragements. But it is preferable to dying of mirage.

Of Mr Niall Sheridan and Mr Donagh MacDonagh I know nothing, except that they have just published 'Twenty Poems' between them; of Miss Irene Haugh, nothing, excpet that she has just published 'The Valley of the Bells', and that her chief concern, in the words of her *Dublin Magazine* reviewer, is God; of Mr Niall Montgomery's poetry, nothing at all.

6. Ex Cathezra

Make It New. By Ezra Pound.

'A collection of reports (in the biologist's sense) on specific bodies of writing, undertaken in the hope, and with the aims, of criticism, and in accordance with the ideogrammic method,' on the Troubadours with special reference to Arnaut Daniel (speech in relation to music), Elizabethan classicists, translators of Greek and the past half-century of French poetry (speech), Henry James and Remy de Gourmont (human consciousness immediately prior to the author's) and Guido Cavalcanti (synthesis of aforementioned in mediaeval Tuscan *virtù* lost and gone for ever), representing Mr Pound's critical activity, *via* discussion, translation, pastiche, music and new composition, in the two great modes of prognosis and excernment, from 1912 to Anno XII. Only the ignoramus will ignore the continuity of these essays, only the reader already familiar with Mr Pound's A B C's of Reading and Economics and — it goes without saying — Ernest Fenollosa's 'Chinese Written Character' will appreciate it thoroughly.

The opening essay has a penetrating account of the deterioration of Provençal poetry after the crusade of 1298. This would have been the very place for a *pronunciamento* on that most fascinating question, the *Minne* modification of *amour courtois*, but it cannot have seemed to Mr Pound at the time. Heinrich von Morungen is invoked in a much later context, his famous Tagelied coming as a great relief after lashings of James. The *Razo* on the luxurious Arnaut is a pleasing piece of informative criticism by pastiche, the translations that follow give a good idea of his *cantabile*.

The essay on the Elizabethans is in the main bouquets for Marlow (with the *e* or without) and Golding (Arthur) as translators, plus objurgations on the beastly bigot Milton. It is notable for an apology to the reader: 'pardon the professional tone whereof I seem unable to divest myself in discussing these matters', and two epigrams. 'Education is an onanism of the soul', 'Beauty is a gasp between clichés.' *Translators of Greek* is boilable down to a plea for more sense and less syntax. Bérard's Homer is not mentioned.

The essay on the French poets is full of acumen and persimmon, and the one most likely to interest the current reader. Laforgue, Corbière and Rimbaud are duly affirmed and discriminated, however debatable the opinion that Corbière is the greatest of these and his *Rapsodie Foraine* (transcribed in full) 'beyond all comment'. The parallels Rimbaud-Cézanne, Corbière-Goya take longer to meet than most. Rimbaud has more tags than Cézanne, *Bateau Ivre* pullulates with them, and they matter no more than Thibaud's slipped notes. Strange that such *sen de trobar* as Mr Pound's should not vibrate to Rimbaud's ironical Hugoisms, also that it should succumb to Gourmont's *Litanies de la Rose* (transcribed in full). There is no mention of Apollinaire, whose *Chanson du Mal Aimé* seems to me worth the whole of the best of Merril, Moréas, Vielé-Griffin, Spire, Régnier, Jammes (all quoted, the last copiously) put together. The best of this essay is in the notes on Romains and Unanimism, stating among other facts not sufficiently received these two of major interest, that Romains *is* Unanimism, and a poet of importance.

The essay on James is, as its author observes, 'a dull grind of an affair'. The suggestion that Fielding was deficient in comprehension of the novel as a form, because we have no notes (no?) from his hand on the subject, is very nice. The 'distinction' on Gourmont is what Renard would call *'bien dumaficelé'*, the extracts that follow spangled with sparklers. The picture of Gourmont as the *uomo singolare* can scarcely be deemed complete in the absence of twentieth century Arlotto, Gonnella, Folengo and Monkey Laocoon.

'Stray Document' is a synopsis of Imagism, together with instructions to the candidate for the poetry certificate. 'Let him dissect the lyrics of Goethe coldly . . .'

Cavalcanti (1910–31), with addenda out of Anno XII, is a most terrific organon. From the text, translation and exegesis of *Donna me pregha* Guido emerges *gran maestro*, not of amor, as the china-maniac Petrarch would insist, but of the entire mediaeval *scibile*, which Mr pound may possibly consider to be the same thing. There is an admirable paean on the 'mediterranean sanity'.

In sum, a galvanic belt of essays, education by provocation, Spartan maieutics. It is no disparagement of Mr Pound to observe that Sidney's 'verse no cause to poetry' has not been ousted, but merely made to move up a little in the bed, by the 'blocks of verbal manifestation'. *Raum für alle* . . . .

7. Papini's Dante

Dante Vivo. By Giovanni Papini. Translated by Eleanor Hammond Broadus and Anna Benedetti.

To these already familiar with the versatility of Signor Papini's middle terms, it will not come as a shock to find him (Chapter I) deriving from the circumstances of his having been born Florentine, embraced Catholicism and written verse, a peculiar aptitude to understand Dante. Nevertheless it is shocking, in its implication that these ingredients, racial, religious and artistic, were as agreeably accommodated in the case of Dante as admittedly they now are in the case of Signor Papini. But it is well known, and Signor Papini himself admits, that Dante's concern with not failing as an artist was so intense as to preclude his devoting himself seriously to succeeding as a citizen, on that *maladetta e sventurata fossa*, or as a devotional mechanic. It could even be sustained that mediocrity in the civic and religious spheres was an important condition of his eminence in the artistic, and Signor Papini himself seems to lean towards this opinion: 'He failed as a statesman, as a White Guelph and as a Ghibelline, as a moral reformer and as a Christian. In recompense he was successful as a poet. But he owes this eminence, at least in part, to the last and gravest of his failures.' This in Chapter XLVIII, after the unqualified assertion in Chapter I that Dante Alighieri, like Signor Papini, was Florentine, Catholic and artist. The copulatives of Signor Papini are as protean as his middles.

The initial confusion distributes itself over the book. Analysis of what a man is not may conduce to an understanding of what he is, but only on condition that the distinction is observed. Signor Papini does not observe it, nor indeed make it, till the book is over. Chapter XLII: 'The greatest wrong one can do to Dante . . . is to classify his most important work as literature.' As what, then? As *morale negotium*, in whole and in part a moral act, demiurgic anagogics, supplement to the Bible, sequel to the

Apocalypse, the work of a prophet partaking of John the Baptist and a haruspex à la Joachim de Flora ('Daniel without the lions, Tarchon without Tages'), announcing the dispensation of the Holy Spirit, that of the Father and the Son having broken down. Relief from this picture may be obtained in Coppée's gazetteer and Nietzsche's hyena.

The same ideology identifies the Veltro (VangElo eTeRnO) with the Paraclete, not to be confused, as the fashion is, with Beatrice's DXV, who is a temporal prince and harbinger of the Veltro. The argument is driven home as follows: 'The expectation of the Paraclete is, even in modern times, more alive among Catholic writers than is generally supposed: it is sufficient to instance Léon Bloy.' More than sufficient.

In the margin of this special pleading the Dante 'raté' is well observed and illustrated. It is pleasant to be reminded that lechery, wrath and pride were his meed of the cardinal sins; that he had a mania for tearing out the hair of his enemies and for applying to his friends and himself formulae usually reserved for the members of the Trinity; that he introjected certain forms of suffering like a neurotic, loathed children, hungered all his life long to be called 'son', and had Ovidian amours by the dozen. Pleasant, but beside the point, inaccessible within its Messianic cocoon, of Dante the artist. The purpose of these marginalia would be the reduction of Dante to lovable proportions. But who wants to love Dante? We want to READ Dante — for example, his imperishable reference (Paolo-Francesca episode) to the incompatibility of the two operations.

8. The Essential and the Incidental

Windfalls. By Sean O'Casey.

What is arguable of a period — that its bad is the best gloss on its good — is equally so of its representatives taken singly. A proper estimate of Molière as master of prose dialogue depends largely on a proper estimate of him as a very humdrum practitioner of the alexandrine — *teste* for example 'La Princesse d'Elide', where the passage from the latter to the former vehicle is one of the great reliefs in literature. Similarly to Chaplin's comic *via* his *mièvre*, Eisenstein's cinematography *via* his Moscow copybook.

This is the interest of 'Windfalls' — that by its juxtaposition of what is distinguished and what is not, the essential O'Casey and the incidental, it facilitates a definition of the former. The volume comprises two sections of verse, a squib on the recruiting campaign in Ireland, four short stories, of which three represent 'an effort to get rid of some of the bitterness that swept into me when the Abbey Theatre rejected "The Silver Tassie",' and two one-act knockabouts. It is in these last that Mr O'Casey comes into his own, and with a distinctness that would be less vivid if he had contrived to get there more quickly.

Mr O'Casey is a master of knockabout in this very serious and honourable sense — that he discerns the principle of disintegration in even the most complacent solidities, and activates it to their explosion. This is the energy of his theatre, the triumph of the principle of knockabout in situation, in all its elements and on all its planes, from the furniture to the higher centres. If 'Juno and the Paycock', as seems likely, is his best work so far, it is because it communicates most fully this dramatic dehiscence, mind and world come asunder in irreparable dissociation — 'chassis' (the credit of having readapted Aguecheek and Belch in Joxer and the Captain being incidental to the larger credit of having dramatized the slump in the human solid). This impulse of material to escape and be consummate in its own knockabout is admirably expressed in the two 'sketches' that conclude this volume, and especially in 'The End of the Beginning', where the entire set comes to pieces and the chief character, in a final spasm of dislocation, leaves the scene by the chimney.

Beside this the poems are like the model palace of a dynamiter's leisure moments. 'Walk with Eros', through the seasons complete with accredited poetic phenomena and emotions to match, is the *ne plus ultra* of inertia, a Walt Disney inspected shot after shot on the celluloid. The influences of nature are great, but they do not enable the disruptive intelligence, exacting the tumult from unity, to invert its function. A man's mind is not a claw-hammer.

The short stories have more jizz, notably (characteristically) that on the dissolution of Mollser, the consumptive girl who had such a good curtain in 'The Plough and the Stars'. Mr O'Casey's admirers will give him the credit of allegorical intention in 'I Wanna Woman'.

But the main business, when at last it is reached, obliterates these preliminaries. And no reader so gentle but must be exalted to forgiveness, even of the prose poems in 'Second Fall', by the passage in 'The End of the Beginning', presenting Messrs Darry Berrill and Barry Derril supine on the stage, 'expediting matters' in an agony of calisthenics, surrounded by the doomed furniture.

9. Censorship in the Saorstat

An act to make provision for the prohibition of the sale and distribution of unwholesome literature and for that purpose to provide for the establishment of a censorship of books and periodical publications, and to restrict the publication of reports of certain classes of judicial proceedings and for other purposes incidental to the aforesaid. (16th July, 1929)

The Act has four parts.

Part 1 emits the definitions, as the cuttle squirts ooze from its cod. E.g., 'the word "indecent" shall be construed as including suggestive of, or inciting to sexual immorality or unnatural vice or likely in any other similar way to corrupt or deprave.' Deputies and Senators can seldom have been so excited as by the problem of how to make the definitive form of this litany orduretight. Tate and Brady would not slip through it now if the Minister for Justice deemed they ought not. A plea for distinction between indecency obiter and ex professo did not detain a caucus that has bigger and better things to split than hairs, the pubic not excepted. 'It is the author's expressed purpose, it is the effect which his thought will have as expressed in the particular words into which he has *flung* (eyetalics mine) his thought that the censor has to consider.' (Minister for Justice)

Part 2 deals with the constitution of and procedure to be adopted by the Censorship of Publications Board, the genesis of prohibition orders, the preparation of a register of prohibited publications and the issuing of search warrants in respect of prohibited publications.

The Board shall consist of five fit and proper persons. This figure was arrived at only after the most animated discussion. Twelve was proposed as likely to form a more representative body. But the representative principle was rejected, notably by Deputy Professor Tierney, who could not bear the thought of

84

any committee with only half a Jew upon it. This is a great pity, as the jury convention would have ensured the sale of at least a dozen copies in this country, assuming, as in reverence bound, that the censors would have gone to bed simultaneously and independently with the text, and not passed a single copy of the work from hand to hand, nor engaged a fit and proper person to read it to them in assembly. 'Fit and proper' would seem to denote nothing less than highly qualified in common sense, 'specialists in common sense' (Dep. Prof. Alton). Dep. J. J. Byrne burst all his buttons in this connexion: 'Give me the man broad-minded and fair who can look at the thing from a common sense point of view. If you want to come to a proper conclusion upon what is for the good of the people in a question of this kind, I unhesitatingly *plump* for the common sense man.' This is getting dangerously close to the opinion of Miss Robey, that for the artist as for the restaurateur the customer is always right. Imagine if you are able, and being able care to, Dep. J. J. Byrne's selection coming to the proper conclusion with reference say to the *Secret Life* of Procopius, a work that has so far evaded the net. His position would be as invidious as that of Jerome reading Cicero, for which he was whipped by the devil in a Lenten dream, were it not that the man broad-minded and fair is at liberty to withdraw his purities from the pollution before they are entirely spent, that is to say almost at once. 'It is not necessary for any sensible individual to read the whole of a book before coming to the conclusion whether the book is good, bad or indifferent.' (Dep. J. J. Byrne) There are books which are so blatantly indecent and known to be indecent that it would be unnecessary for the members of the Board to read every line of them. Should the members of the Board, for instance, be compelled to read through every line of *Ulysses*, a book that has been universally condemned?' (Minister for Justice). The judicial outlook. Dep. J. J. Byrne's censor's Lenten dream will not wake him.

The stock allusion to the *Decameron* caused no little flutter in the Senate, but was skilfully negotiated by Senator Johnson: 'I do not think it has any great reputation as a book, and so with regard to many other books', and by the Minister for Justice: 'some of Boccaccio's stories, I understand, are quite excellent, e.g., the plaintive tale of Patient Griselda.'

The Bill as originally drafted provided for complaints to be made with reference to obscene publications via recognized associations, something in the style of the Irish Commercial Travellers' Federation, a kind of St Vincent de Paul de Kock Societies. In so far as this clause was spewed out of the Dail and actually not reinserted p.r. by the Senate, any individual is now in theory entitled to lodge a complaint on his own bottom. But as this would entail his procuring five copies of the work for submission to the Board, he finds himself obliged, precisely as the original Bill intended, to cast around for some body whose interest in the public state of mind condones, more amply than his own, a small outlay. And behold the Catholic Truth Society, transformed into an angel of light, stands at his right hand. Precisely as the original Bill intended.

The Register of Prohibited Publications is a most happy idea, constituting as it does, after the manner of Boston's Black Book, a free and permanent advertisement of those books and periodicals in which, be their strictly literary status never so humble, inheres the a priori excellence that they have annoyed the specialist in common sense. I may add that it is the duty of every customs official in the Saorstat to exhibit on demand this Register to the incoming mug.

Part 3 sets forth with loving care the restrictions on publication of reports of judicial proceedings. No longer may the public lap up the pathological titbit or the less frigid proceedings for divorce, nullity of marriage, judicial separation and restitution of conjugal rights. No sports less indoor than these engross, even in our evening papers, such space as survives the agitation of protective tariffs, subsidies, monopolies and quotas and the latest snuffles from the infant industries at Drogheda, Navan, Dundalk, Mullingar, Westport, Edenderry, Slane, Ennis, Athy, Newbridge, Nenagh, Portarlington, Tuam, Mallow, Thurles (two syllables), Arklow, Aughrim, Portlaw, Killaloe, Enniscorthy, Carrickmacross, Carrick-on-Suir, Ballyboghill and Bray, e.o.o.e.

Part 4 enshrines the essence of the Bill and its exciting cause, in the general heading tactfully enveloped among the 'other purposes incidental', the prohibition namely of publications advocating the use of contraceptives, blushing away beyond the endurance of the most dogged reader among the Miscellaneous and General. France may commit race suicide, Erin will never.

86

And should she be found at any time deficient in Cuchulains, at least it shall never be said that they were contraceived. Thus to waive the off chance of a reasonable creature is no longer a mere mortal sin, but a slapup social malfeasance, with corollary in the civic obligation to throttle reason itself whenever it happens to be 'flung' into a form obnoxious to the cephalopods of state. The pure Gael, drawing his breath from his heels, will never be permitted to defile his mind with even such fairly clean dirt as the *Black Girl in her Search for God* so long as he can glorify his body to the tune of half a dozen byblows, white as pthisis, in search for a living. This yoke will not irk him.

Such is the cream of a measure that the Grand Academy of Balnibarbi could hardly have improved on. Even if it worked, which needless to say it does not, it would do so gratis, an *actum agere* regardless of expense. For the Irish are a characteristic agricultural community in this, that they have something better to do than read and that they produce a finished type of natural fraudeur having nothing to learn from the nice discriminations of Margaret Sanger and Marie Carmichael Stopes, D. Sc., Ph. D., F. R. S. Litt., etc. Doubtless there is something agreeable to the eye in this failure to function to no purpose, the broken handpump in the free air station. Paley's watch in the desert is charming, but the desert in Paley's watch still more so. Whether a government of the people by the people can afford these free shows is another matter.

Finally to amateurs of morbid sociology this measure may appeal as a curiosity of panic legislation, the painful tension between life and thought finding issue in a constitutional belch, the much reading that is a weariness exorcised in 21 sections. Sterilization of the mind and apotheosis of the litter suit well together. Paradise peopled with virgins and the earth with decorticated multiparas.

The Register as on the 30th September 1935 shows 618 books and 11 periodicals under the ban. Among men, women and for all I know children of letters writing in English, the most liberally advertised are: Aldous Huxley, the Powys brothers, Maugham, John Dos Passos, Aldington, Sinclair Lewis, Wyndham Lewis, William Faulkner, D. H. Lawrence, Wells, Chaucer (Eve), Kay Boyle, Middleton Murry and Mae West. Irish authors deemed from time to time unwholesome are: O'Flaherty, O'Casey,

O'Leary, O Faolain (no apostrophe), Shaw, Clarke and Moore (George). Foreign writers distinguished in all English versions are: Döblin, both Zweigs, Gaston Leroux, Gorki, Leonhard Frank, Roth, Rolland, Romains, Barbusse, Schnitzler, Hamsun, Colette, Casanova, Céline, all contributors to the Spanish Omnibus, Jarry, Boccaccio, Dékobra and the incomparable Vicki. With regard to scientific works it need only be said that all the most up to date enchiridions both of marriage and of love are here, from Bertrand Russell's to Ralph de Pomerai's. Of the banned periodicals perhaps the most keenly missed have been, pending the expiration (if any) of the Prohibition Order: *Ballyhoo*, *Health and Efficiency*, *Broadway and Hollywood Movies*, *Health and Strength*, *Empire News*, *incorporating the Umpire*, *Thompson's Weekly*, and *True Romances*.

My own registered number is 465, number four hundred and sixty-five, if I may presume to say so.

We now feed our pigs on sugarbeet pulp. It is all the same to them.

10. An Imaginative Work!

The Amaranthers. By Jack B. Yeats.

The chartered recountants take the thing to pieces and put it together again. They enjoy it. The artist takes it to pieces and makes a new thing, new things. He must. Mr Jack Yeats is an artist. *The Amaranthers* is art, not horology. Ariosto to Miss — *absit nomen!*

The moments are not separate, but concur in a single process: analytical imagination. Not first the old slum coming down, then the new slum going up, but in a single act slum seen as it is and other. 'The effect of the Innkeeper, framed with white lace, red ribbons running up like rays to the left and right of him, with the water dripping from his forelock, over the penthouses of his brows, was bold.' As discovered it is bold. Or awkwardness in a bar: 'One or two lifted their hats lightly, or ironically, from their heads. One took off the grey kid gloves he was wearing, blew into them and put them away. One bent a light cane into a half hook, then let it spring up and caught it in his palm.' Who has seen with this light, or irony, since — *abest nomen.*

The irony is Ariostesque, as slight and as fitful and struck from the same impact, between the reality of the imagined and reminiscence of its elements. The face remains grave, but the mind has smiled. The profound *risolino* that does not destroy.

The discontinuity is Ariostesque, proceeding from the same necessary indifference to flowers on the table-centre on the centre of the table, from the same respect for the mobility and autonomy of the imagined (a world of the same order if not so intense as the 'ideal real' of Prowst, so obnoxious to the continuity girls). Of the two themes, in whose coalescence the book ends, the Amaranthers and James Guilfoyle, the first is invaded by the play in the 'Hope On', then dropped for a hundred pages; and the second broken into three by the episodes of Ohoh and Pensamiento. An imaginative adventure does not enjoy the same corsets as a reportage.

There is no allegory, that glorious double-entry, with every credit in the said account a debit in the meant, and inversely; but the single series of imaginative transactions. The Island is not throttled into Ireland, nor the City into Dublin, notwithstanding 'one immigrant, in his cups, recited a long narrative poem'.

There is no symbol. The cream horse that carries Gilfoyle and the cream coach that carries Gilfoyle are related, not by rule of three, as two values to a third, but directly, as stages of an image.

There is no satire. Believers and make-believers, not Gullivers and Lilliputians; horses and men, not Houyhnhnms and Yahoos; imaginative fact, beyond the fair and the very fair. 'God is good, so why not Brown?'

The landscape is superb, radiant and alive, with its own life, not the hikers'. There was a stage 'suggestion' in the *Old Sea Road*: 'The sky, sea and land are brighter than the people.'

The end, the beginning, is among the hills, where imagination is not banned, and Gilfoyle saying to the Amaranthers, their cowering skyscraper days over: 'You begin to stop emptying your heads, every time they begin to fill with thoughts, and then you will begin to think, and then you will stop thinking and begin to talk. . . . And then you will stop talking and begin to fancy, and then you will stop fancying and begin to imagine. And by that time it will be morning.' He has been through it, and so he knows.

11. Intercessions by Denis Devlin

With himself on behalf of himself. with his selves on behalf of his selves. Tour d'ébène.

Which is a relief now that verse is most conveniently to be derided (or not) at the cart-tail of faction or convulsed on the racks of disaffected metres or celebrating the sects, schisms and sectiuncles that have had all the poets they are likely to want in this world at least. The relief of poetry free to be derided (or not) on its own terms and not in those of the politicians, antiquaries (Geleerte) and zealots.

But the poets have always played push-pin in the country of Bentham.

Its own terms, that is terms of need, not of opinion, still less of faction; opinion being a response to and at least (at best) for a time an escape from need, from one kind of need, and art, in this case these poems, no more (!) than the approximately adequate and absolutely non-final formulation of another kind. Art has always been this — pure interrogation, rhetorical question less the rhetoric — whatever else it may have been obliged by the 'social reality' to appear, but never more freely so than now, when social reality (*pace* ex-comrade Radek) has severed the connexion.

As between these two, the need that in its haste to be abolished cannot pause to be stated and the need that is the absolute predicament of particular human identity, one does not of course presume to suggest a relation of worth. Yet the distinction is perhaps not idle, for it is from the failure to make it that proceeds the common rejection as 'obscure' of most that is significant in modern music, painting and literature. On the one hand the 'Unbefriedigt jeden Augenblick', the need to need ('aimant l'amour'), the art that condenses as inverted spiral of need, that condenses in intensity and brightness from the mere need of the angels to that of the seraphinns, whose end is its own end in the end and the source of need:

> Let me be always in this state of grace
> Keep me going on bribes like this, the unfinished
>   handwork of sunset
> Be to me also for a sign
> Of burgled outhouses round an inviolable family stone
> As a priest uncertain among his mysteries when a bending
>   candle-flame provokes forbidden images.

And on the other the go-getters, the gerimandlers, Davus and the morbid dread of sphinxes, solution clapped on problem like a snuffer on a candle, the great crossword public on all its planes: 'He roasteth roast and is satisfied. Yea, he warmeth himself and saith, Aha, I am warm.'

The only suggestions therefore that the reviewer may venture without impertinence are such as have reference to this fundamental. Thus he may suggest the type of need (Braque's is not Munch's, neither's is Klee's, etc.), its energy, scope, adequacy of expression, etc. There seems no other way in which this miserable functionary can hope to achieve innocuity. Unless of course he is a critic.

The Dives-Lazarus symbiosis, as intimate as that of fungoid and algoid in lichen (to adopt the Concise New Oxford Dictionary example). Here scabs, lucre, etc., there torment, bosom, etc., but both here and there *gulf*. The absurdity, here or there, of either without the other, the inaccessible other. In death they did not cease to be divided. Who predeceased? A painful period for both.

This Gospel *conte cruel* is taken to suggest the type of dilemma that caused these poems to be written. It is stated with the bareness of an initial theme in what I take to be the earliest in date: *Est Prodest*.

> Frightened antinomies!
> I have wiped examples from mirrors
> My mirror's face and I
> Are like no god and me
> My death is my life's plumed gnomon.

This is the type, the identity made up of cathexes not only multivalent but interchangeable, the 'multiplicate netting/ Of lives distinct and wrangling/ Each knot all other's potential.'

This position formulated in *Est Prodest* with the singleness of a melodic line recurs at various degrees of tension and elaboration in the other poems that compose this volume (with the possible exception of *Bacchanal* and *Argument with Justice*, which appear to belong to a different and in the terms of this simplification very much less interesting order of experience) but nowhere with such passionate intricacy as in *Communication from the Eiffel Tower*, where it is developed round the superb dream *bisticcio*: Gobethou-Gobenow, through its fundamental modes of love, death, act and thought, to the most remarkable adequacy and finality of expression.

> Apprehension becomes china eyes become
> A wavering plainchant trappist digging his gravesods
> One sod per diem, and he stiffens as the vivid sweat
> Stings in the roots of his hair.
> Under the pierlamps cold wind and leavetaking and sad eyes
> Other side of the gangway always . . .
> A boy embittered when summer rain smells fresh on hot
>   limbs and
> Desire trapped in a girl's wet hair breathes
> Or a bored mechanic polishing and he mutters
> Caught by sight of his face in one of a million rollers
> Or the bewilderment of the strong and fair covertly noting
> A beloved forehead suave as styles of a maize becoming
> Restless and stained
> Or no news yet from emigrant sons . . .
> Night my pure identity that breathe
> One in all breaths, absorber of all breaths
> Night that gestate in symbol-troubled women,
> Dumb breeders of being
> Wombed in your cathedrals let us watch
> Till the forgotten matutinal colours flame
> Various the rosewindows through . . .

If I knew of any recent writing to compare with this I should not do so.

If only the 8 in the last line had been left on its side. So: ∞

Apart from this major poem, related to those that lead up to and away from it very much as Apollinaire's *Chanson du Mal-Aimé* to the other *Alcools*, and with the exceptions suggested above, the insistence with which the ground invades the surface throughout is quite extraordinary. Extraudenary. Passages which even on a fourth or fifth reading seemed to sag, as even the most competent linkwriting is bound to sag, eventually tighten into line with those of more immediate evidence. This was very forcibly my experience with the third stanza of *Gradual*, adduced in the *Times Lit. Sup.*, in a tone of exhausted disapproval, as indicating mental confusion and technical ineptitude.

It is naturally in the image that this profound and abstruse self-consciousness first emerges with the least loss of integrity. To cavil at Mr Devlin's form as overimaged (the obvious polite cavil) is to cavil at the probity with which the creative act has carried itself out, a probity in this case depending on a minimum of rational interference, and indeed to suggest that the creative act should burke its own conditions for the sake of clarity.

The time is perhaps not altogether too green for the vile suggestion that art has nothing to do with clarity, does not dabble in the clear and does not make clear, any more than the light of day (or night) makes the subsolar, -lunar and -stellar excrement. Art is the sun, moon and stars of the mind, the whole mind. And the monacodologists who think of it in terms of enlightenment are what Nashe, surprised by a cordial humour, called the Harveys, 'the sarpego and sciatica of the Seven Liberall Sciences.'

First emerges. With what directness and concreteness the same totality may be achieved appears from the exquisite last stanza of *The Statue and the Perturbed Burghers*, which with its repetition of 'crimson and blind' and the extraordinary evocation of the unsaid by the said has the distinction of a late poem by Hölderlin (e.g. 'Ihr lieblichen Bilder im Tale. . .'):

> The tendrils of fountain water thread that silk music
> From the hollow of scented shutters
> Crimson and blind
> Crimson and blind
> As though it were my sister
> Fireflies on the rosewood
> Spinet playing
> With barely escaping voice
> With arched fastidious wrists to be so gentle.

Mr Denis Devlin is a mind aware of its luminaries.

12. MacGreevy on Yeats

This is the earliest connected account of Mr Yeats's painting. To it future writers on the subject will, perhaps, be indebted, no less than writers on Proust to Madariaga's essay, or writers on Joyce to Curtius's — indebted for an attitude to develop, or correct, or reject. It is rare for the first major reaction to art of genius to come, as here, from a compatriot of the artist. The causes of this are no doubt profound and forcible. It is agreeable to find them coerced.

The greater part of this essay was written in London, in 1938. A postscript, written this year in Ireland, covers Mr Yeats's development from 1938 to the present day. The past seven years have confirmed Mr MacGreevy in the views that a dozen London publishers, not yet so fortunate as to lack paper, declined to publish. This is not to be wondered at. It is difficult to formulate what it is one likes in Mr Yeats's painting, or indeed what it is one likes in anything, but it is a labour, not easily lost, and a relationship once started not likely to fail, between such a knower and such an unknown.

There is at least this to be said for mind, that it can dispel mind. And at least this for art-criticism, that it can lift from the eyes, before *rigor vitae* sets in, some of the weight of congenital prejudice. Mr MacGreevy's little book does this with a competence that will not surprise those who have read his essay on Mr Eliot, or his admirable translation of Valery's *Introduction à la Méthode de Léonard de Vinci*, nor those who follow, in the *Record*, his articles on writers and artists little known, as yet, in the Republic.

The National Painter

Mr MacGreevy sees in Mr Yeats the first great painter, the first great Irish painter, that Ireland has produced, or indeed, could have produced; the first to fix, plastically, with completeness and for his time finality, what is peculiar to the Irish scene and to the Irish people. This is the essence of his interpretation, and it permeates the essay in all its parts. The position is made clear at the outset:

> . . . What was unique in Ireland was that the life of the people considered itself, and was in fact, spiritually and culturally as well as politically, the whole life of the nation. Those who acted for the nation officially were outside the nation. They had a stronger sense of identity with the English governing class than with the people of Ireland, and their art was no more than a province of English art. The first genuine artist, therefore, who so identified himself with the people of Ireland as to be able to give true and good and beautiful artistic expression to the life they lived, and to that sense of themselves as the Irish nation, inevitably became not merely a *genre* painter like the painters of the *petit peuple* in other countries, and not merely a nation's painter in the sense of Pol de Limbourg, Louis le Nain, Bassano, Ostade or Jan Steen were national painters, but *the* national painter in the sense that Rembrandt and Velasquez and Watteau were national painters, the painter who in his work was the consummate expression of the spirit of his own nation at one of the supreme points in its evolution.

This, the Constable and Watteau analogies, the statement of the political backgrounds to the first (until about 1923) and the second periods, the elucidations of 'Helen' and 'The Blood of Abel', seem to me art-criticism of a high order, indeed. They constitute an affirmation of capital importance, not only for those who feel in this way about mr Yeats, or for those who as yet feel little or nothing about Mr Yeats, but also for those, such as myself, who feel in quite a different way about Mr Yeats.

The Artist

The national aspects of Mr Yeats's genius have, I think, been over-stated, and for motives not always remarkable for their aesthetic purity. To admire painting on other than aesthetic grounds, or a painter, *qua* painter, for any other reason than that he is a good painter, may seem to some uncalled for. And to some also it may seem that Mr Yeats's importance is to be sought elsewhere than in a sympathetic treatment (how sympathetic?) of the local accident, or the local substance. He is with the great of our time, Kandinsky and Klee, Ballmer and Bram van Velde, Rouault and Braque, because he brings light, as only the great dare to bring light, to the issueless predicament of existence, reduces the dark where there might have been, mathematically at least, a door. The being in the street, when it happens in the room, the being in the room when it happens in the street, the turning to gaze from land to sea, from sea to land, the backs to one another and the eyes abandoning, the man alone trudging in sand, the man alone thinking (thinking!) in his box — these are characteristic notations having reference, I imagine, to processes less simple, and less delicious, than those to which the plastic *vis* is commonly reduced, and to a world where Tir-na-nOgue makes no more sense than Bachelor's Walk, nor Helen than the apple-woman, nor asses than men, nor Abel's blood than Useful's, nor morning than night, nor inward than the outward search.

B. SELF

1. The Possessed

[*We are given to understand that the following is a reply to our reporter's criticism of the M. L. S. Plays; as such we publish it.* — Ed. T. C. D.]

Ladies and Gentlemen!
On my left, torturing his exquisite Pindaric brolly, the Divine Marquis of Stanfor (cries of 'What?' 'Whom?' 'Never!'). On my right and slightly to my rere, ineffably manipullulating his celebrated tipstaff, his breastfallen augs sorrowfully scouring the arena for two snakes in the grass, Professor Giovannino Allcon, direct from the Petites Maisons. Order gentlemen please! This is a respectable stadium. These are two honest boys. Ladies! Ladies! This unprecedented contest — shall I say competition? — is timed to begin from one minute to another. Silence for the mal sacré. Now please.

Stanfor: Telephus and treachery!

Allcon: I spy a Guy
with the G. P. I.
passing woeful
in a B. A. shroud.

S. (*rending stays from his umbrella, torn by the violence of his epileptical intimations*):
How square, O Lord, how square!
Kiss me Stanley.
Tom's in his hedge
creeping and peeping.
Doom in a desert!

A. (*clenching the caducceus*):
I am from the North,
from Bellyballaggio
where they never take their hurry

minxing marriage in their flaxmasks
omygriefing and luvvyluvvyluvving and wudiftheycudling
from the fourth or fifth floor of their hemistitched hearts
right and left of the Antrim Road.
That's why I like him
Ulster my Hulster!
Daswylyim! *(Weeps.)*

S. *(Postponing inarticulation)*:
In the chiarinoscurissimo
I was unable to distinguish the obvious balloons.
The Infanta might have cantered
like a shopwalker
through the Dämmerung
but she was not in training.
The Cid (or hero, whose death, we understand, occurred
in 1199)
could have been transmitted with a seriousness
more in keeping with the spiritual ancestor of the centre-
forward.
A production, Professor,
from every centre of perspective
vox populi and yet not
platotudinous
cannot entertain
me.

A. *(bravely sustaining the impact of his refracted imaginings)*:
O saisons! o châteaux!
I will play now a little song on my good grand.
I will be very, very heartily
too, too fascinating
on my sickroom aelopantalion
Purchè por —
ti la gonnel —
la
or a Godsent Dumka at prima vista
inspired in the early morning
by the Marquise de Brinvilliers.
O the bitter giggle and the grand old cramp

of a cold heart and a good stomach!
O saisons! o châteaux!

S.   Wheat barley beans lentils millet fitches.

A.   Shall we prepare our bread therewith?

S.   When the cows come home
when the cows come home.

A.   And consider the case of a lesser known author?

2. On Murphy

Excerpt from a letter of July 17, 1936 to Thomas McGreevy

The point you raise is one that I have given a good deal of thought to. Very early on, when the mortuary and Round Pond scenes were in my mind as the necessary end, I saw the difficulty and danger of so much following Murphy's own 'end'. There seemed two ways out. One was to let the death have its head in a frank climax and the rest be definitely epilogue (by some such means as you suggest. I thought for example of putting the game of chess there in a section by itself). And the other, which I chose, and tried to act on, was to keep the death subdued and go on as coolly and finish as briefly as possible. I chose this because it seemed to me to consist better with the treatment of Murphy throughout, with the mixture of compassion, patience, mockery and 'tat twam asi' that I seem to have directed on him throughout, with the sympathy going so far and no further (then losing patience) as in the short statement of his mind's fantasy on itself. There seemed to me always the risk of taking him too seriously and separating him too sharply from the others. As it is I do not think the mistake (Aliosha mistake) has been altogether avoided. A rapturous recapitulation of his experience following its 'end' woud seem to me exactly the sort of promotion that I want to avoid: and an ironical one is I hope superfluous. I find the mistake in the mortuary scene, which I meant to make more rapid but which got out of hand in the dialogue. Perhaps it is saved from anticlimax by presence of M. all through. I felt myself he was liable to recur in his grotesque person until he was literally one with the dust. And if the reader feels something similar it is what I want. The last section is just the length and speed I hoped, but the actual end doesn't satisfy me very well.

3. On Murphy

Excerpt from a letter of November 13, 1936 to George Reavey

Let me say at once that I do not see *how* the book can be cut without being disorganized. Especially if the beginning is cut (and God knows the first half is plain sailing enough). The latter part will lose such resonance as it has. I can't imagine what they want me to take out. I refuse to touch the section entitled *Amor Intellectualis quo M. se ipsum amat*. And I refuse also to touch the game of chess. The horoscope chapter is also essential. But I am anxious for the book to be published and therefore cannot afford to reply with a blank refusal to anything.

Will you therefore communicate . . . my extreme aversion to removing one-third of my work proceeding from my extreme inability to understand how this can be done and leave a remainder? But add that if they would indicate precisely what they have in mind, and the passages that cause them pain, I should be willing to suppress such passages as are not essential to the whole and adjust such others as seem to them a confusion of the issue. . . . Do they not understand that if the book is slightly obscure it is because it is a compression and that to compress it further can only result in making it more obscure? The wild and unreal dialogues, it seems to me, cannot be removed without darkening and dulling the whole thing. They are the comic exaggeration of what elsewhere is expressed in elegy, namely, if you like, the Hermeticism of the spirit. Is it here that they find the 'skyrockets'? There is no time and no space in such a book for *mere* relief. The relief has also to do work and reinforce that from which it relieves. And of course the narrative is hard to follow. And of course deliberately so.

4. On Works to 1951

10.IV.51

Cher Monsieur Lindon,

Bien reçu ce matin votre lettre d'hier. Je vous remercie vivement de votre généreuse avance.[1]

J'ai fait faire la photo cet après-midi. Je l'aurai après-demain et vous l'enverrai aussitôt.

Je sais que Roger Blin veut monter la pièce.[2] Il devait demander une subvention à cet effet. Je doute fort qu'on la lui accorde. Attendons *Godot*, mais pas pour demain.

La nouvelle dont la première moitié, sous le titre *Fuite*, a paru dans *les Temps modernes*, est à votre disposition.[3] Cela peut-il attendre jusqu'à mon retour? C'est mon premier travail en français (en prose). *Le Calmant* que Madame Dumesnil a remis à Monsieur Lambrichs, ferait peut-être mieux l'affaire.[4] Ce sera à votre choix.

Je suis très content que vous ayez envie d'arriver rapidement à *L'Innommable*. Comme je vous l'ai dit, c'est à ce dernier travail que je tiens le plus, quoiqu'il m'ait mis dans de sales draps. J'essaie de m'en sortir. Mais je ne m'en sors pas. Je ne sais pas si ça pourra faire un livre. Ce sera peut-être un temps pour rien.[5]

Laissez-moi vous dire encore combien je suis touché par l'intérêt que vous portez à mon travail et par le mal que vous vous donnez pour le défendre. Et croyez à mes sentiments sincèrement amicaux.

Samuel Beckett

---

1. La 'généreuse avance' en question se montait, je crois me rappeler, à 25 000 anciens francs.
2. Il s'agissait d'*En attendant Godot* à Paris. Les théâtres refusèrent longtemps cette pièce où il n'y avait 'ni femme, ni communiste, ni curé'. La générale eut lieu finalement en janvier 1953.
3. *Les Temps modernes* en avaient interrompu la publication après la première

livraison. Cette nouvelle parut sous le titre 'La Fin' dans *Nouvelles et Textes pour rien*.

4.   Georges Lambrichs était alors secrétaire du comité de lecture des Editions de Minuit. 'Le Calmant' est également paru dans *Nouvelles et textes pour rien*.

5.   De fait, ces tentatives parurent ensuite sous le titre *Textes pour rien*.

5. On Endgame

Extracts from Correspondence with Director Alan Schneider

December 27, 1955

Dear Alan:
If I don't get away by myself now and try to work I'll explode, or implode. So I have retreated to my hole in the Marne mud and am struggling with a play. Yours,

Sam

January 11, 1956

Success and failure on the public level never mattered much to me, in fact I feel much more at home with the latter, having breathed deep of its vivifying air all my writing life up to the last couple of years. . . . When in London the question arose of a new production [of Beckett's 'Waiting for Godot'], I told the [producers] that if they did it my way they would empty the theatre. . . . For the moment all I can say and all I want to say is that this Miami fiasco [the Florida production of 'Godot'] does not distress me in the smallest degree, or only in so far as it distresses you.

P. S. I am writing an even worse affair and have got down the gist of the first act (of two).

April 12, 1956

Afraid no plays to show you. I did finish another, but don't like it. It has turned out a three-legged giraffe, to mention only the architectonics, and leaves me in doubt whether to take a leg off or add one on.

June 21, 1956

I have no clear picture of the [New York] production [of 'Godot'].

Much seems to get across, but to the exclusion of too much else, probably. . . . Have at last written another, one act, longish, hour and a quarter I fancy. Rather difficult and elliptic, mostly depending on the power of the text to claw, more inhuman than 'Godot'. My feeling, strong, at the moment, is to leave it in French for a year at least. . . . I'm in a ditch somewhere near the last stretch and would like to crawl up on it.

October 15, 1956

I don't in my ignorance agree with the round and feel 'Godot' needs a very closed box. . . . Have begun to work on the new play with Blin and Martin [Roger Blin, French director of 'Godot' and director and star of 'Endgame', and Jean Martin, who played Lucky and Clov in the Paris productions of 'Godot' and 'Endgame']. A very long one act, over an hour and a half I shd think. . . . I am panting to see the realization and know if I am on some kind of road, and can stumble on, or in a swamp.

April 16, 1957

I can't face my typewriter these days, so you'll have to make the best you can of my foul fist. We created 'Fin de Partie' ('Endgame') at the Royal Court in London. We go on here at the end of the month at the Studio des Champs-Élysées. 'Fin de Partie' is very difficult to get right. Perhaps I have the wrong idea as to how it should be done. Blin and Martin have done a very good job — in spite of me! And the work in London improves our chances here.

April 30, 1957

I have not even begun the translation. I have until August to finish it and keep putting off the dreaded day. . . . It seems funny to be making plans for a text which does not yet exist and which, when it does, will inevitably be a poor substitute for the original (the loss will be much greater than from the French to the English 'Godot'). . . . We opened here last Friday at the Studio des Champs-Élysées. . . . The reactions so far are good and I have not much misgiving as to the outcome. Blin, after a shaky start in

London, is now superb as Hamm. I have nothing but wastes and wilds of self-translation before me for many miserable months to come.

P. S. I quite agree that my work is for the small theatre. The Royal Court is not big, but 'Fin de Partie' gains unquestionably in the greater smallness of the Studio.

August 12, 1957

I have finished translation and am sending it to Barney [Barney Rosset of the Grove Press] today. . . . Now it's up to Barney and you — if your interest survives a reading of the script. Whatever the two of you decide is, in advance, O.K. with me.

The creation in French at the Royal Court [the London production of 'Endgame' had been done in French] was rather grim, like playing to mahogany, or rather teak. In the little Studio des Champs-Élysées the hooks went in. . . . It would be fine if you get over to see it. You know by experience what little help I am with my own work and I have little or no advice for you. But simply to see the production here, for which I am very grateful, while not altogether agreeing, might be of some use to you.

September 30, 1957

If you want to be absolutely sure of seeing this production, you need to arrive on the 10th at latest and in time to get to the Avenue Montaigne by 21 hours GMT approx. . . . I think it would help you considerably to see it. . . . In any case you'll have the great benefit of seeing me and getting another dose of my stutterings.

October 26, 1957

It was good seeing you. Sorry I wasn't of more help about the play but the less I speak of my work the better. The important thing was for you to see the production.

December 29, 1957

It would be impertinent of me to advise you about the article you are doing and I don't intend to. But when it comes to journalists I feel the only line is to refuse to be involved in exegesis of any kind. And to insist on the extreme simplicity of dramatic situation and issue. If that's not enough for them, and it obviously isn't, it's plenty for us, and we have no elucidations to offer of mysteries that are all of their making. My work is a matter of fundamental sounds (no joke intended) made as fully as possible, and I accept responsibility for nothing else. If people want to have headaches among the overtones, let them. And provide their own aspirin. Hamm as stated, and Clov as stated, together as stated, nec tecum nec sine te, in such a place, and in such a world, that's all I can manage, more than I could.

January 9, 1958

I received . . . yesterday jacket of book and extracts from our letters, with no indication of what the latter was for. This disturbed me as I do not like publication of letters . . . I shd prefer the letters not to be used unless [it is] important for you that they should be. I see from your letter that it is and this is simply to say all right, go ahead. . . . I have refused to allow the prayer passage to be touched in London and my feeling is it must not be. More tomorrow and thanks for all your efforts. I like ashcan ad.

February 6, 1958

This in haste to thank you for your letter with programme and the reviews which I here do solemnly declare well up to standard. I do hope . . . that you and your actors — to whom my warm greetings — will be repaid for all your work and enthusiasm by a reasonable canter. . . . I am so glad you have been able to preserve the text in all its impurity.

March 4, 1958

'Endspiel' in Roger Blin's mise en scène opens in Vienna day after tomorrow, in a small new theatre (Theater am Fleischmarkt). Alternance with Ionesco, Genet and Ghelderode, so I'm in good company. Genet's new play, 'Les Nègres', is very fine. . . .

Hope the flu has gone. Write when you have a moment. Salutations to Jean [Mrs Schneider] and to my niece [3-year-old Vicky Schneider]. Ever,

— Sam

6. On Play

To George Devine

Paris 9.3.64

Dear George

The last rehearsals with Serreau have led us to a view of the *da capo* which I think you should know about. According to the text it is rigorously identical with the first statement. We now think it would be dramatically more effective to have it express a slight weakening, both of question and of response, by means of less and perhaps slower light and correspondingly less volume and speed of voice. To consider only strength of light and voice, if we call C the minimum and A the maximum the first time round we would get something like this:

I

C	Opening chorus
A	First part of I.
B	Second part of I.

II

Less than C	Second chorus.
B or B plus	First part of II.
C or C plus	Second part of II.

III

C or C plus

The impression of falling off which this would give, with suggestion of conceivable dark and silence in the end, or of an indefinite approximating toward it, would be reinforced if we obtained also, in the repeat, a quality of hesitancy, of both question and answer, perhaps not so much in a slowing down of actual débit as in a less confident movement of spot from one face to another and less immediate reaction of the voices. The whole idea involves a spot mechanism of greater flexibility than has seemed necessary so far. The inquirer (light) begins to emerge as no less a victim of his inquiry than they and as needing to be free, within narrow limits, literally to act the part, i.e. to vary if only slightly his speeds and intensities. Perhaps some form of manual control after all.

This is all new and will yield more as we go into it. Thought I had better submit it to you without delay.

See you Monday. If they could be word perfect by then it would be marvellous. Love to Jocelyn,
yours ever,

Sam

7. On Murphy

Paris 14. 6. 67

Dear Sigle Kennedy

Please forgive unforgivable delay in answering your letter.

I don't have thoughts about my work. So don't be upset if my answer to your question is no. It is not a reasoned one. I simply do not feel the presence in my writings as a whole of the Joyce & Proust situations you evoke. If I were in the unenviable position of having to study my work my points of departure would be the 'Naught is more real . . .' and the 'Ubi nihil vales . . .' both already in *Murphy* and neither very rational.

Bon courage quand même.

Sincerely

(signed) Sam. Beckett

8. On Endgame

Zwei Fragen:
1. Als *Endspiel* vor zehn Jahren zum ersten Mal aufgeführt wurde, hinterliess das Stück bei einem grosses Teil des Publikums das Gefühl der Ratlosigkeit. Man fand, dass den Zuschauern Rätsel aufgegeben würden, deren Lösung auch der Autor nicht wisse. Glauben Sie, dass *Endspiel* den Zuschauern Rätsel aufgibt?
2. Sind Sie der Meinung, dass der Autor eine Lösung der Rätsel parat haben muss?

Zwei Antworten von Samuel Beckett:
1. *Endspiel* wird blosses Spiel sein. Nichts weniger. Von Rätseln und Lösungen also kein Gedanke. Es gibt für solches ernstes Zeug Universitäten, Kirchen, Cafés du Commerce usw.
2. Der dieses Spieles nicht.

Part III

Words About Painters

1. Geer van Velde

Born the third of four April 5th 1898 at Lisse near Leyden. Tulips and Rembrandt. 1911 apprenticed to a house-painter. Wanderings in Holland and Brabant, rubbing colours in order to buy them. Since 1925 in Paris. 1927 South of France. 1931 Brittany. Exhibitions; 1925 at the Hague, 1926–30 in Paris with Independants. 1933 with his brother Bram van Velde at the Hague, 1937 at the Hague, Pictures in Amsterdam in the Stedelijk and the Regnault collection, at the Hague in the Stedelijk and the Kramers collection, in private collections in Brabant, France, Germany, U.S.A. and even England.

Believes painting should mind its own business, *i.e.* colour. *i.e.* no more say Picasso than Fabritius, Vermeer. Or inversely.

2. La peinture des van Velde ou le Monde et le Pantalon

LE CLIENT: Dieu a fait le monde en six jours, et vous, vous n'êtes pas foutu de me faire un pantalon en six mois.

LE TAILLEUR: Mais Monsieur, regardez le monde, et regardez votre pantalon.

Pour commencer, parlons d'autre chose, parlons de doutes anciens, tombés dans l'oubli, ou résorbés dans des choix qui n'en ont cure, dans ce qu'il est convenu d'appeler des chefs-d'oeuvre, des navets et des oeuvres de mérite.

Doutes d'amateur, bien entendu, d'amateur bien sage, tel que les peintres le rêvent, qui arrive les bras ballants et les bras ballants s'en va, la tête lourde de ce qu'il a cru entrevoir. Quelle rigolade les soucis de l'exécutant, à côté des affres de l'amateur, que notre iconographie de quatre sous a gavé de dates, de périodes, d'écoles, d'influences, et qui sait distinguer, tellement il est sage, entre une gouache et une aquarelle, et qui de temps en temps croit deviner ce qu'il aime, tout en gardant l'esprit ouvert. Car il s'imagine, le pauvre, que rien de ce qui est peinture ne doit lui rester étranger.

Ne parlons pas de la critique proprement dite. La meilleure, celle d'un Fromentin, d'un Grohmann, d'un McGreevy, d'un Sauerlandt, c'est de l'Amiel. Des hystérectomies à la truelle. Et comment en serait-il autrement? Peuvent-ils seulement citer? Quant Grohmann démontre chez Kandinsky des réminiscences du graphique mongol, quand McGreevy rapproche si justement Yeats de Watteau, où vont les rayons? Quand Sauerlandt se prononce, avec finesse et — soyons justes — parcimonie, sur le cas du grand peintre inconnu qu'est Ballmer, où cela retombe-t-il? *Das geht mich nicht an*, disait Ballmer, que les écrits de Herr Heidegger faisaient cruellement souffrir. Il le disait fort modestement.

Ou alors on fait de l'esthétique générale, comme Lessing. C'est un jeu charmant.

Ou alors on fait de l'anecdote, comme Vasari et Harper's Magazine.

Ou alors on fait des catalogues raisonnés, comme Smith.

Ou alors on se livre franchement à un bavardage désagréable et confus. C'est le cas ici.

Avec les mots on ne fait que se raconter. Eux-mêmes les lexicographes se déboutonnent. Et jusque dans le confessional on se trahit.

Ne pourrait-on attenter à la pudeur ailleurs que sur ces surfaces peintes presque toujours avec amour et souvent avec soin, et qui elles-mêmes sont des aveux? Il semble que non. Les copulations contre nature sont très cotées, parmi les amateurs du beau et du rare. Il n'y a qu'à s'incliner devant le savoir-vivre.

Achevé, tout neuf, le tableau est là, un non-sens. Car ce n'est encore qu'un tableau, il ne vit encore que de la vie des lignes et des couleurs, ne s'est offert qu'à son auteur. Rendez-vous compte de sa situation. Il attend, qu'on le sorte de là. Il attend les yeux, les yeux qui, pendant des siècles, car c'est un tableau d'avenir, vont le charger, le noircir, de la seule vie qui compte, celle des bipèdes sans plumes. Il finira par en crever. Peu importe. On le rafistolera. On le rabibochera. On lui cachera le sexe et on lui soutiendra la gorge. On lui foutra un gigot à la place de la fesse, comme on l'a fait pour la Vénus de Giorgione à Dresde. Il connaîtra les caves et les plafonds. On lui tombera dessus avec des parapluies et des crachats, comme on l'a fait pour le Lurçat à Dublin. Si c'est une fresque de cinq mètres de haut sur vingt-cinq de long, on l'enfermera dans une serre à tomates, ayant préalablement eu le soin d'en aviver les couleurs avec de l'acide azotique, comme on l'a fait pour le *Triomphe de César* de Mantegna à Hampton Court. Chaque fois que les Allemands n'auront pas le temps de le déménager, il se transformera en champignon dans un garage abandonné. Si c'est un Judith Leyster on le donnera à Hals. Si c'est un Giorgione et qu'il soit trop tôt pour le donner encore au Titien, on le donnera à Dosso Dossi (Hanovre). Monsieur Berenson s'expliquera dessus. Il aura vécu, et répandu de la joie.

Ceci explique pourquoi les tableaux ont tellement meilleure mine au musée que chez le particulier.

Ceci explique pourquoi le *Chef-d'OEuvre Inconnu* de Balzac est à tant de chevets. L'oeuvre soustraite au jugement des hommes finit par expirer, dans d'effroyables supplices. L'oeuvre considérée comme création pure, et dont la fonction s'arrête avec la genèse, est vouée au néant.

Un seul amateur (éclairé) l'aurait sauvé. Un seul de ces messieurs au visage creusé par les enthousiasmes sans garantie, aux pieds aplatis par des stations innombrables, aux doigts usés par des catalogues à cinquante francs, qui regardent d'abord de loin, ensuite de près, et qui consultent du pouce, dans les cas particulièrement épineux, le relief de l'impasto. Car il n'est pas question ici de l'animal grotesque et méprisable dont le spectre hante les ateliers, comme celui du tapir les turnes normaliennes, mais bien de l'inoffensif loufoque qui court, comme d'autres au cinéma, dans les galeries, au musée et jusque dans les églises avec l'espoir — tenez-vous bien — de jouir. Il ne veut pas s'instruire, le cochon, ni devenir meilleur. Il ne pense qu'à son plaisir.

C'est lui qui justifie l'existence de la peinture en tant que chose publique.

Je lui dédie les présents propos, si bien faits pour l'obnubiler davantage.

Il ne demande qu'à jouir. L'impossible est fait pour l'en empêcher.

L'impossible est fait notamment pour que des tranches entières de peinture moderne lui soient tabou.

L'impossible est fait pour qu'il choisisse, pour qu'il prenne parti, pour qu'il accepte à priori, pour qu'il rejette à priori, pour qu'il cesse de regarder, pour qu'il cesse d'exister, devant une chose qu'il aurait pu simplement aimer, ou trouver moche, sans savoir pourquoi.

On lui dit:

'Ne vous approchez pas de l'art abstrait. C'est fabriqué par une bande d'escrocs et d'incapables. Ils ne sauraient faire autre chose. Ils ne savent pas dessiner. Or, Ingres a dit que le dessin est la probité de l'art. Ils ne savent pas peindre. Or, Delacroix a dit que la couleur est la probité de l'art. Ne vous en approchez pas. Un enfant en ferait autant.'

Qu'est-ce que ça peut lui faire, que ce soient des escrocs, s'ils lui procurent du plaisir? Qu'est-ce que ça peut lui faire, qu'ils ne sachent pas dessiner? Cimabue savait-il dessiner? Qu'est-ce que ça veut dire: savoir dessiner? Qu'est-ce que ça peut lui faire, que les enfants puissent en faire autant? Qu'ils en fassent autant. Ce sera merveilleux. Qu'est-ce qui les en empêche? Leurs parents peut-être. Ou n'en auraient-ils pas le temps?

On lui dit:

'Ne perdez pas votre temps avec les réalistes, avec les sur-réalistes, avec les cubistes, avec les fauves, avec les apprivoisés, avec les impressionistes, avec les expressionistes, etc., etc. Et chaque fois on lui donne des raisons excellentes. Il s'en faut de peu qu'on ne lui dise de ne pas s'acoquiner avec les déplorables siècles de peinture précézannienne.

On lui dit:

'Tout ce qui est bon en peinture, tout ce qui est viable, tout ce que vous pouvez admirer sans crainte, se trouve sur une ligne qui va depuis les grottes des Eyzies jusqu'à la Galerie de France.'

On ne précise pas si c'est une ligne préétablie ou si c'est un tracé qui se déroule au fur et à mesure comme la bave de la limace. On ne lui montre pas à quels signes il peut savoir si un tableau donné s'y rattache. C'est une ligne invisible. Serait-ce par hasard un plan, leur ligne?

On lui dit:

'N'a le droit d'abandonner l'expression directe que celui qui en est capable. La peinture à déformation est le refuge de tous les ratés.'

Droit! Depuis quand l'artiste, comme tel, n'a-t-il pas tous les droits, c'est-à-dire aucun? Il lui sera peut-être bientôt interdit d'exposer, voire de travailler, s'il ne peut justifier de tant d'années d'académie.

D'identiques bêlements saluaient, il y a 150 ans, le vers libre et la gamme par tons.

On lui dit:

'Picasso, c'est du bon. Vous pouvez y aller avec confiance.'

Et il n'entendra plus les ronflements homériques.

On lui dit, avec une grande bonté:

'Tout est objet pour la peinture, sans excepter les états d'âme, les rêves et même les cauchemars, à condition que la transcription en soit faite avec des moyens plastiques.'

Serait-ce par hasard l'emploi ou le non-emploi de ces engins qui déciderait de la présence ou de l'absence, sur la ligne précitée, d'un tableau donné?

Il serait en tout état de cause utile, et même intéressant, de savoir ce qu'on entend par moyens plastiques. Or, personne ne le saura jamais. C'est une chose que seuls les initiés subodorent.

Mais supposons que la définition en soit acquise, une fois pour toutes, de telle sorte que n'importe quel chassieux pourra s'écrier, devant le tableau à juger: 'C'est bien, les moyens sont plastiques', et qu'il soit établi, en même temps, que seule est bonne la peinture qui s'en sert. Que dire, en ce cas, de l'artiste qui y renoncerait?

Ceci soulève de vastes et ténébreux problèmes d'esthétique pratique, je parle de ceux ayant trait au pompier, à l'hypopompier, à l'hyperpompier et au pompier de propos délibéré, à leurs rapports réciproques et zones de clivage, et d'une manière générale à la légitimité, pardon, à l'opportunité, de la malfaçon créatrice voulue.

On lui dit:

'Dali, c'est du pompier. Il ne saurait faire autre chose.'

Voilà ce qui s'appelle ne rien laisser au hasard. On étrangle d'abord, puis on éventre.

Les jugements jumelés prospèrent en ce moment. Ils en disent long sur les juges.

Je propose le spécimen ci-dessus comme modèle du genre. Il est court, clair, bien balancé (affirmation d'abord, négation ensuite), gentiment transcendantal, facile à prononcer pour les anglo-saxons et sans réplique. C'est-à-dire qu'il faudrait commencer la réplique vers l'âge de quinze ans, au plus tard.

Il n'y aurait pas trop de dix volumes d'analyses nauséabondes pour en extirper l'énorme et malin malentendu, celui qui empoisonne depuis si longtemps, sur le plan de l'idée, les rapports entre peintres, entre amateurs, entre peintres et amateurs.

Car si ce n'est pas Dali, c'est un autre; et si ce n'est pas pompier, c'est autre chose.

Voyons seulement quelques-unes des questions qui se posent, quand nous aurons admis que pompier a un sens et que Dali, volontairement ou involontairement, en présente les flétrissures.

Pourquoi ne ferait-il pas du pompier, délibérément, si cela fait son affaire?

Ne peut-on concevoir le pompier et le non-pompier réunis, celui-là au service de celui-ci? La prose de la *Princess d'Elide* serait-elle aussi belle, s'il n'y avait pas les vers? Les paysages de Claude ne doivent-ils vraiment rien au staffage?

Comment peut-on savoir qu'il ne saurait faire autre chose? A-t-il signé un procès-verbal dans ce seans? Le fait qu'il n'a jamais fait autre chose? Et pourquoi n'aurait-il pas fait du pompier, rien que du pompier, depuis sa plus tendre enfance, si cela faisait son affaire?

Et pourquoi, ne sachant faire que du pompier, n'en tirerait-il pas une chose admirable? Parce que pompier admirable est une *contradictio in adjecto*? Le fut.

Et ainsi de suite.

Voilà une infime partie de ce qu'on dit à l'amateur.

On ne lui dit jamais:

'Il n'y a pas de peinture. Il n'y a que des tableaux. Ceux-ci, n'étant pas des saucisses, ne sont ni bons ni mauvais. Tout ce qu'on peut en dire, c'est qu'ils traduisent, avec plus ou moins de pertes, d'absurdes et mystérieuses poussées vers l'image, qu'ils sont plus ou moins adéquats vis-à-vis d'obscures tensions internes. Quant à décider vous-même du degré d'adéquation, il n'en est pas question, puisque vous n'êtes pas dans la peau du tendu. Lui-même n'en sait rien la plupart du temps. C'est d'ailleurs un coefficient sans intérêt. Car pertes et profits se valent dans l'économie de l'art, où le tu est la lumière du dit, et toute présence absence. Tout ce que vous saurez jamais d'un tableau, c'est combien vous l'aimez (et à la rigueur pourquoi, si cela vous intéresse). Mais cela non plus vous ne le saurez probablement jamais, à moins de devenir sourd et d'oublier vos lettres. Et le temps viendra où, de vos visites au Louvre, car vous n'irez plus qu'au Louvre, il ne vous restera que des souvenirs de durée: "Suis resté trois minutes devant le sourire du Professeur Pater, à le regarder".'

Voilà une infime partie de ce qu'on ne dit jamais à l'amateur. Ce n'est manifestement pas plus vrai que le reste. Mais cela le changerait.

La peinture (puisqu'il n'y en a pas) d'Abraham et Gerardus van Velde est peu connue à Paris, c'est-à-dire peu connue. Ils y travaillent pourtant depuis vingt ans, depuis seize ans.

Celle d'A. van Velde est particulièrement peu connue. Ses tableaux ne sont pour ainsi dire jamais sortis de l'atelier, à moins que ne compte comme sortie l'annuelle aération tête en bas aux Indépendants. De cette longue réclusion ils émergent, aujourd'hui, aussi frais que s'ils n'avaient jamais cessé, depuis leurs débuts, d'être admirés, tolérés et vilipendés.

Aucune exposition, même modeste, n'a jamais rassemblé à Paris les toiles soit de l'un, soit de l'autre.

Par contre, une importante exposition G. van Velde a eu lieu à Londres, en 1938, à la Galerie Guggenheim Jeune. Étrange rencontre. De nombreuses toiles de lui sont restées en Angleterre.

Ils ont travaillé surtout á Paris et dans ses abords immédiats. A. van Velde a cependant séjourné en Corse (1929-31) et Majorque (1932-36).

J'allais oublier le plus important. A. van Velde est né à La Haye en Octobre 1895. Ce fut l'instant des brumes. G. van Velde est né près de Leyde, en Avril 1897. Ce fut l'instant des tulipes.

Ce qui suit ne sera qu'une défiguration verbale, voire un assassinat verbal, d'émotions qui, je le sais bien, ne regardent que moi. Défiguration, à bien y penser, moins d'une réalité affective que de sa risible impreinte cérébrale. Car il suffit que je refléchisse à tous les plaisirs que me donnaient, à tous les plaisirs que me donnent, les tableaux d'A. van Velde, et à tous les plaisirs que me donnaient, à tous les plaisirs que me donnent, les tableaux de G. van Velde, pour que je les sente m'échapper, dans un éboulement innombrable.

Donc, un double massacre.

Quant à la forme elle aura forcément les allures d'une suite de propositions apodictiques. C'est la seule manière de ne pas se mettre en avant.

Il importe tout d'abord de ne pas confondre les deux oeuvres. Ce sont deux choses, deux séries de choses, absolument distinctes. Elles s'écartent, de plus en plus, l'une de l'autre. Elles s'écarteront, de plus en plus, l'une de l'autre. Comme deux hommes qui, partis de la Porte de Chatillon, s'achemineraient, sans trop bien connaître le chemin, avec de fréquents arrêts pour se donner du courage, l'un vers la Rue Champ-de-l'Alouette, l'autre vers l'Ile des Cygnes.

Il importe ensuite d'en bien saisir les rapports. Qu'ils se ressemblent, deux hommes qui marchent vers le même horizon, au milieu de tant de couchés, d'assis et de transportés en commun.

Parlons d'abord de l'aîné. Son originalité est, des deux, de loin la plus facile à saisir, la plus éclatante. La peinture de G. van Velde est excessivement réticente, agit par des irradiations que l'on sent défensives, est douée de ce que les astronomes appellent (sauf erreur) une grande vitesse d'échappement. Tandis que celle d'A. van Velde, semble figée dans un vide lunaire. L'air l'a quittée.

J'exagère.

Je pense surtout aux dernières toiles, celles que G. van Velde vient de rapporter du Midi, celles qu'A. van Velde a faites à Paris en 40 et 41 (il n'a rien fait depuis). Le contraste se faisait moins sentir il y a dix ans. Mais il éclatait déjà.

Cette distribution des rôles est des plus inattendues. Tout laissait prévoir l'inverse. Et j'ai bien peur que nous n'allions vers des constatations qui devront les renverser en effet, pour tout esprit soucieux de cohérence.

D'où vient cette impression de chose dans le vide? De la façon? C'est comme si l'on disait que l'impression de bleu vient du ciel. Cherchons un cercle plus ample.

Nous avons affaire chez Abraham van Velde à un effort d'aperception si exclusivement et farouchement pictural que nous autres, dont les réflexions sont tout en murmures, ne le concevons qu'avec peine, ne le concevons qu'en l'entraînant dans une sorte de ronde syntaxique, qu'en le plaçant dans le temps.

(Je note, littéralement entre parenthèses, le curieux effet, dont j'ai été témoin plus d'une fois, que produisent ces tableaux sur le spectateur de bonne foi. Ils le privent, même le plus prompt au commentaire, de l'usage de la parole. Ce n'est point un silence de bouleversé, à en juger par les éloquentes réfutations qui finissent quand même par couler. C'est un silence, on dirait presque de convenance, comme celui qu'on garde, tout en se demandant pourquoi, devant un muet.)

Écrire aperception purement visuelle, c'est écrire une phrase dénuée de sens. Comme de bien entendu. Car chaque fois qu'on veut faire faire aux mots un véritable travail de transbordement, chaque fois qu'on veut leur faire exprimer autre chose que des mots, ils s'alignent de façon à s'annuler mutuellement. C'est, sans doute, ce qui donne à la vie tout son charme.

Car il ne s'agit nullement d'une prise de conscience, mais d'une prise de vision, d'une prise de vue tout court. Tout court! Et d'une prise de vision au seul champ qui se laisse parfois voir sans plus, qui n'insiste pas toujours pour être mal connu, qui accorde par moments à ses fidèles d'en ignorer tout ce qui n'est pas apparence: au champ intérieur.

Espace et corps, achevés, inaltérables, arrachés au temps par le faiseur de temps, à l'abri du temps dans l'usine à temps (qui passait sa journée dans le Sacré-Coeur pour ne plus avoir à le voir?), voilà ce qui vaut bien Barbizon et le ciel de la Pérouse. C'en est, d'ailleurs, dans un sens, l'aboutissement.

Les oiseaux sont tombés, Manto se tait, Tirésias ignore.

Ignorance, silence et l'azur immobile, voilà la solution de la devinette, la toute dernière solution.

Pour d'aucuns.

A quoi les arts représentatifs se sont-ils acharnés, depuis toujours? A vouloir arrêter le temps, en le représentant.

Que de vols, de courses, de fleuves, de flèches. Que de chutes et d'ascensions. Que de fumée. Nous avons eu jusqu'au jet d'urine (brebis du divin Potter), symbole par excellence de la fuite des heures.

Nous n'en serons jamais assez reconnaissants.

Mais il était peut-être temps que l'objet se retirât, par ci par là, du monde dit visible.

Le 'réaliste', suant devant sa cascade et pestant contre les nuages, n'a pas cessé de nous enchanter. Mais qu'il ne vienne plus nous emmerder avec ses histoires d'objectivité et de choses vues. De toutes les choses que personne n'a jamais vues, ses cascades sont assurément les plus énormes. Et s'il existe un milieu où l'on ferait mieux de ne pas parler d'objectivité, c'est bien celui qu'il sillonne, sous son chapeau parasol.

La peinture d'A. van Velde serait donc premièrement une peinture de la chose en suspens, je dirais volontiers de la chose morte, idéalement morte, si ce terme n'avait pas de si fâcheuses associations. C'est-à-dire que la chose qu'on y voit n'est plus seulement représentée comme suspendue, mais strictement telle qu'elle est, figée réellement. C'est la chose seule, isolée par le besoin de la voir, par le besoin de voir. La chose immobile dans le vide, voilà enfin la chose visible, l'objet pur. Je n'en vois pas d'autre.

La boîte crânienne a le monopole de cet article.

C'est là que parfois le temps s'assoupit, comme la roue du compteur quand la dernière ampoule s'éteint.

C'est là qu'on commence enfin á voir, dans le noir. Dans le noir qui ne craint plus aucune aube. Dans le noir qui est aube et midi et soir et nuit d'un ciel vide, d'une terre fixe. Dans le noir qui éclaire l'esprit.

C'est là que le peintre peut tranquillement cligner de l'oeil.

Nous sommes loin du fameux 'droit' de la peinture de créer ses objets. C'est le plein air qui appelle cette opération audacieuse.

Loin également des bambochades du surréel.

Des rapports d'outillage avec la grande école de peinture critique-critique de ses objets, critique de ses moyens, critique de ses buts, critique de sa critique, et dont nous ne sommes encore qu'aux magnificences siennoises.

Il y avait une fois un homme qu'on appelait le grand Thomas. . . .

Inutile de chercher l'originalité d'A. van Velde ailleurs que dans cette objectivité prodigieuse, car tout le reste s'y rattache, non certes comme conséquence, ni comme effet, mais dans le sens que la même occasion l'a suscité. Je parle de tout ce que cette peinture présente d'irraisonné, d'ingénu, de non-combine, de mal-léché.

Impossible de raisonner sur l'unique. La peinture raisonnée, c'est celle dont chaque touche est une synthèse, chaque ton l'élu d'entre mille, chaque trait symbole, et qui s'achève dans des tortillements d'enthymème. C'est la nature morte au papillon. C'est la machine à coudre sur la table d'opération. C'est la figure vue de face et de profil à la fois. C'est sans doute aussi la dame aux seins dorsaux, quoique ceci ne soit pas certain. Elle produit des chefs-d'oeuvre à sa façon.

Impossible de vouloir autre l'inconnu, l'enfin vu, dont le centre est partout et la circonférence nulle part; ni le seul agent capable de le faire cesser; ni le but, qui est de le faire cesser. Car c'est bien de cela qu'il s'agit, de ne plus voir cette chose adorable et effrayante, de rentrer dans le temps, dans la cécité, d'aller s'ennuyer devant les tourbillons de viande jamais morte et frissonner sous les peupliers. Alors on la montre, de la seule façon possible.

Impossible de mettre de l'ordre dans l'élémentaire.

On la montre ou on ne la montre pas.

La peinture conjecturale lui a fourni l'outil. Son emprise ne va pas plus loin. Cet outil, A. van Velde l'a bien modifié depuis. On n'en sent pas moins la provenance. Il l'a adapté aux besoins de son travail, lequel n'a rien de conjectural.

Il y a des Braque qui ressemblent à des méditations plastiques sur les moyens mis en oeuvre. D'où cette étrange impression d'hypothèse qui s'en dégage. Le définitif est toujours pour demain. Il semble que cette remarque soit pertinente pour une grande partie, et non la moindre, de ce qu'on appelle la peinture moderne vivante.

Chez A. van Velde, rien de pareil. Il affirme. Même pas. Il constate. Ses moyens ont la spécificité d'un spéculum, n'existent que par rapport à leur fonction. Il ne s'y intéresse pas suffisament pour en douter. Il ne s'intéresse qu'à ce qu'ils reflètent.

Nous touchons ici à quelque chose de fondamental et qui pourrait permettre de saisir en vertu du quoi exactement il existe, depuis Cézanne, toute une peinture coupée de ses antécédents (que de temps elle a perdu en voulant s'y rattacher), et en vertu de quoi, à son tour, la peinture d'A. van Velde se détache de celle-ci.

L'art adore les sauts.

Passer de cette fidélité massive à la peinture de G. van Velde, c'est passer de l'*Homme au Heaume* à la *Vue de Delft*, de la Sixtine aux Loges (je compare des rapports).

C'est un passage difficile.

Que dire de ces plans qui glissent, ces contours qui vibrent, ces corps comme taillés dans la brume, ces équilibres qu'un rien doit rompre, qui se rompent et se reforment à mesure qu'on regarde? Comment parler de ces couleurs qui respirent, qui halètent? De cette stase grouillante? De ce monde sans poids, sans force, sans ombre?

Ici tout bouge, nage, fuit, revient, se défait, se refait. Tout cesse, sans cesse. On dirait l'insurrection des molécules, l'intérieur d'une pierre un millième de seconde avant qu'elle ne se désagrège.

C'est ça, la littérature.

Il serait préférable de ne pas s'exposer à ces deux façons de voir et de peindre, le même jour. Du moins dans les premiers temps.

Mettons la chose plus grossièrement. Achevons d'être ridicule.

A. van Velde peint l'étendue.

G. van Velde peint la succession.

Puisque, avant de pouvoir voir l'étendue, à plus forte raison avant de pouvoir la représenter, il faut l'immobiliser, celui-là se détourne de l'étendue naturelle, celle qui tourne comme une toupie sous le fouet du soleil. Il l'idéalise, en fait un sens interne. Et c'est justement en l'idéalisant qu'il a pu la réaliser avec cette objectivité, cette netteté sans précédent. C'est là sa trouvaille. Il la doit à un besoin tendu à l'extrême de voir clair.

Celui-ci, au contraire, est entièrement tourné vers le dehors, vers le tohu-bohu des choses dans la lumière, vers le temps. Car on ne prend connaissance du temps que dans les choses qu'il agite, qu'il empêche de voir. C'est en se donnant entièrement au dehors, en montant le macrocosme secoué par les frissons du temps, qu'il se réalise, qu'il réalise l'homme si l'on préfère, dans ce qu'il a de plus inébranlable, dans sa certitude qu'il n'y a ni présent ni repos. C'est la représentation de ce fleuve où, selon le modeste calcul d'Héraclite, personne ne descend deux fois.

C'est un drôle de *memento mori*, la peinture radieuse de G. van Velde. Je le note en passant.

Aucun rapport avec la peinture à montre à arrêt, celle qui, pour avoir accordé aux nénuphars deux minutes par jour pendant l'éternite du psalmiste, croit avoid bloqué la rotation terrestre, sans parler des ennuyeux gigotements des astres inférieurs. Chez G. van Velde le temps galope, il l'éperonne avec une sortie de frénésie de Faust à rebours.

'Voila ce que nous sommes' disent ses toiles. Et elles ajoutent: 'C'est une chance'.

Avec cela c'est une peinture d'un calme et d'une douceur extraordinaires. Décidément, je n'y comprends rien. Elle ne fait pas de bruit. Celle de A. van Velde fait un bruit très caractérisé, celui de la porte qui claque au loin, le petit bruit sourd de la porte qu'on vient de faire claquer à l'arracher du mur.

Deux oeuvres en somme qui semblent se réfuter, mais qui en fait se rejoignent au coeur du dilemme, celui même des arts plastiques: Comment représenter le changement?

Ils se sont refusés, chacun à sa façon, aux biais. Ils ne sont ni musiciens, ni littérateurs, ni coiffeurs. Pour le peintre, la chose est impossible. C'est d'ailleurs de la représentation de cette impossibilité que la peinture moderne a tiré une bonne partie de ses meilleurs effets.

Mais ils n'ont ni l'un ni l'autre ce qu'il faut pour tirer parti plastiquement d'une situation plastique sans issue.

C'est qu'au fond la peinture ne les intéresse pas. Ce qui les intéresse, c'est la condition humaine. Nous reviendrons là-dessus.

Qu'est-ce qu'il leur reste, alors, de représentable, s'ils renoncent à représenter le changement? Existe-t-il quelque chose, en dehors du changement, qui se laisse représenter?

Il leur reste, à l'un la chose qui subit, la chose qui est changée; à l'autre la chose qui inflige, la chose qui fait changer.

Deux choses qui, dans le détachement, l'une du bourreau, l'autre de la victime, où enfin elles deviennent représentables, restent à créer. Ce ne sont pas encore des choses. Cela viendra. En effet.

Ce sont là deux attitudes profondément différentes, et dont les principes hâtivement érigés en antithèse font les délices de la psychologie depuis toujours, depuis les *dyskoloi* et les *eukoloi*. Elles ont leurs racines dans la même expérience. Voilà ce qui est charmant. N'est-ce pas?

L'analyse de cette divergence, si elle n'explique rien, aidera peut-être à situer les deux oeuvres, l'un vis-à-vis de l'autre. Elle pourra éclairer notamment l'écart qu'ils accusent au point de vue style, écart dont il importe de pénétrer le sens profond si l'on veut éviter d'y fonder une confrontation toute en surface. On ne saurait trop y insister. Cette espèce de négligence catégorique, qui traduisent si bien, chez l'aîné, l'urgence et la primauté de la vision intérieure, deviendraient, chez l'autre, des fautes irréparables. Car celui-ci n'a pas affaire à la chose seule, coupée de ses amarres avec tout ce qui en faisait un simple échantillon de perdition, on dirait coupée de ses amarres avec elle-même, et dont le renflouement exige précisément ce mélange de maîtrise et d'ennui, mais à un objet infiniment plus complexe. A vrai dire, moins à un objet qu'à un processus, un processus senti avec une telle acuité qu'il en a acquis une solidité d'hallucination, ou d'extase. Il a affaire toujours au composé. Ce n'est plus le composé naturel, blotti dans ses mornes chatoiements quotidiens, mais les mêmes éléments restent en présence. Confronté par ce bloc impénétrable, A. van Velde l'a fait sauter, pour en libérer ce dont il avait besoin. Pour l'autre, cette solution était d'avance exclue.

Les deux choses devaient rester associées. Car on ne représente la succession qu'au moyen des états qui se succèdent, qu'en imposant à ceux-ci un glissement si rapide qu'ils finissent par se fondre, je dirais presque par se stabiliser, dans l'image de la succession même. Forcer l'invisibilité foncière des choses extérieures jusqu'à ce que cette invisibilité elle-même devienne chose, non pas simple conscience de limite, mais une chose qu'on peut voir et faire voir, et le faire, non pas dans la tête (les peintres n'ont pas de tête, lisez donc canevas à la place, ou estomac, aux endroits où je les en affuble), mais sur la toile, voilà un travail d'une complexité diabolique et qui requiert un métier d'une souplesse et d'une légèreté extrêmes, un métier qui insinue plus qu'il n'affirme, qui ne soit positif qu'avec l'évidence fugace et accessoire du grand positif, du seul positif, du temps qui charrie.

Existe-t-il, derrière ces barbouillages, un solide fonds de trucs pour tromper l'oeil? Sauraient-ils tracer l'arc-en-ciel sans l'aide du compas? Prêter, que dis-je, donner du relief au cul d'un cheval emballé, sous la pluie? Je ne leur ai jamais demandé.

La peinture des van Velde a d'autres secrets, qu'il serait facile de réduire (à l'impuissance) au moyen de ce qui précède. Mais je n'entends pas tout perdre.

Je n'ignore pas combien de tels développements doivent paraître arbitraires, schématiques et peu conformes aux images qui en furent l'occasion et l'aliment, aux images des images. Leur conférer des airs plus décents, plus persuasifs, à grand renfort de restrictions et de nuances, ne serait pas impossible sans doute. Mais ce n'est pas la peine.

Il n'a d'ailleurs été question à aucun moment de ce que font ces peintres, ou croient faire, ou veulent faire, mais uniquement de ce que je les vois faire.

Je tiens à le répéter, de crainte qu'on ne les prenne pour des cochons d'intellectuels.

Or on ne peut concevoir une peinture moins intellectuelle que celle-ci.

A. van Velde, en particulier, ne doit commencer à se rendre compte de ce qu'il a fait qu'environ dix ans après. Entendons-nous. Il sait chaque fois que ça y est, à la façon d'un poisson de haute mer qui s'arrête à la bonne profondeur, mais les raisons lui en sont épargnées.

Cela semble vrai aussi pour G. van Velde, avec les restrictions (nous y voilà) qu'impose son attaque si différente.

Ils me font penser à ce peintre de Cervantès qui, à la demande 'Que peignez-vous?', répondait: 'Ce qui sortira de mon pinceau'.

Pour finir parlons d'autre chose, parlons de l' 'humain'.

C'est là un vocable, et sans doute un concept aussi, qu'on réserve pour les temps des grands massacres. Il faut la pestilence, Lisbonne et une boucherie religieuse majeure, pour que les êtres songent à s'aimer, à foutre la paix au jardinier d'à côté, à être simplissimes.

C'est un mot qu'on se renvoie aujourd'hui avec une fureur jamais égalée. On dirait des dum-dum.

Cela pleut sur les milieux artistiques avec une abondance toute particulière. C'est dommage. Car l'art ne semble pas avoir besoin du cataclysme, pour pouvoir s'exercer.

Les dégâts sont considérables déjà.

Avec 'ce n'est pas humain', tout est dit. A la poubelle.

Demain on exigera de la charcuterie qu'elle soit humaine.

Cela, ce n'est rien. On a quand même l'habitude.

Ce qui est proprement épouvantable, c'est que l'artiste lui-même s'en est mis.

Le poète qui dit: Je ne suis pas un homme, je ne suis qu'un poète. Vite le moyen de faire rimer amour et congés payés.

Le musicien qui dit: Je donnerai la sirène à la trompette bouchée. Ça fera plus humain.

Le peintre qui dit: Tous les hommes sont frères. Allons, un petit cadavre.

Le philosophe qui dit: Protagoras avait raison.

Ils sont capables de nous démolir la poésie, la musique, la peinture et la pensée pendant 50 ans.

Surtout ne protestons pas.

Voulez-vous de l'existant sortable? Mettez-lui un bleu. Donnez-lui un sifflet.

L'espace vous intéresse? Faisons-le craquer.

Le temps vous tracasse? Tuons-le tous ensemble.

La beauté? L'homme réuni.

La bonté? Étouffer.

La vérité? Le pet du plus grand nombre.

Que deviendra, dans cette foire, cette peinture solitaire, solitaire de la solitude qui se couvre la tête, de la solitude qui tend les bras?

Cette peinture dont la moindre parcelle contient plus d'humanité vraie que toutes leurs processions vers un bonheur de mouton sacré.

Je suppose qu'elle sera lapidée.

Il y a les conditions éternelles de la vie. Et il y a son coût. Malheur à qui les distinguera.

Après tout on se contentera peut-être de huer.

Quoi qu'il en soit, on y reviendra.

Car on ne fait que commencer à déconner sur les frères van Velde.

J'ouvre la série.

C'est un honneur.

3. Peintres de l'Empêchement

J'ai dit tout ce que j'avais à dire sur la peinture des frères van Velde dans le dernier numéro des Cahiers d'Art (à moins qu'il n'y en ait eu un autre depuis). Je n'ai rien à ajouter à ce que j'ai dit à cet endroit. C'était peu, c'était trop, et je n'ai rien à y ajouter. Heureusement il ne s'agit pas de dire ce qui n'a pas encore été dit, mais de redire, le plus souvent possible dans l'espace le plus réduit, ce qui a été dit déjà. Sinon on trouble les amateurs. Cela d'abord. Et la peinture moderne est déjà assez troublante en elle-même sans qu'on veuille la rendre plus troublante encore, en disant tantôt qu'elle est peut-être ceci, tantôt qu'elle est peut-être cela. Ensuite on se trouble soi-même, sans nécessité. Et on est déjà assez troublé, de nécessité, et non seulement par la peinture moderne, sans vouloir se troubler davantage, en essayant de dire ce qui n'a pas encore été dit, à sa connaissance. Car céder à l'ignoble tentation de dire ce qui n'a pas encore été dit, à sa connaissance, c'est s'exposer à un grave danger, celui de penser ce qui n'a pas encore été pensé, qu'on sache. Non, ce qui importe, si l'on ne veut pas ajouter à son trouble et à celui des autres devant la peinture moderne et autres sujets de dissertation, c'est d'affirmer quelque chose, que ce soit sans précédent ou avec, et d'y rester fidèle. Car en affirmant quelque chose et y restant fidèle, quoi qu'il arrive, on peut finir par se faire une opinion sur presque n'importe quoi, une bonne opinion bien solide capable de durer toute la vie. Et les opinions de cette sorte, faites pour résister aux siècles, ne sont pas à dédaigner, ne le furent sans doute jamais, même au premier Moyen Âge. Et cela semble être tout particulièrement vrai des opinions ayant trait à la peinture moderne, sur laquelle il n'est pas possible de s'en faire une, même fragile, par les méthodes ordinaires. Mais en affirmant, un beau jour, avec fermeté et puis encore le lendemain, et le surlendemain, et tous les jours, de la peinture moderne qu'elle est ceci, et ceci seulement, alors dans l'espace de dix, douze ans on saura ce que c'est que la peinture moderne, peut-être même assez bien pour pouvoir en faire profiter ses amis, et sans avoir eu à passer le meilleur de ses loisirs dans des soi-disant galeries, étroites, encombrées et mal éclairées, à l'interroger des yeux. C'est-à-dire que l'on saura tout ce qu'il y a à savoir sur la formule adoptée, ce qui constitue la fin de toute science. Savoir ce qu'on veut dire, voilà la sagesse. Et le meilleur moyen de savoir ce qu'on veut dire, c'est de vouloir dire la même chose tous les jours, avec patience, et de se familiariser ainsi avec la formule employée, dans tous ses sables mouvants. Jusqu'à ce que finalement, aux colles classiques sur l'expressionnisme, l'abstraction, le constructivisme, le néo-plasticisme et leurs antonymes, les réponses se fassent tout de suite, complètes, définitives et pour ainsi dire machinales. La sécurité esthétique et le sentiment de bien-être qui en résultent se laissent avantageusement étudier dans la société des peintres modernes eux-mêmes, qui vous diront, pour peu qu'on le leur demande, et même sans qu'on leur demande rien, en quoi exactement la peinture moderne consiste, et en quoi exactement elle ne consiste pas, mais de préférence en quoi exactement elle ne consiste pas, à toute heure du jour et de la nuit, et qui réduiront à néant tout ce qui résiste à cette démonstration en moins de temps qu'il ne leur en faut pour décrire un cercle, ou un triangle. Et leur peinture proprement dite, qu'il ne faut tout de même pas confondre avec leur conversation, porte avec allégresse la même marque de certitude et d'irréfragabilité. A tel point que des deux choses, la toile et le discours, il n'est pas toujours facile de savoir laquelle est l'oeuf et laquelle la poule.

Nous apprenons à l'heure qu'il est, non seulement par la bouche des crocodiles habituels, un oeil plein de larmes et l'autre vissé sur le marché, mais par celle des connaisseurs les plus sérieux et respectables, que l'École de Paris (sens à déterminer) est finie ou presque, que ses maîtres sont morts ou mourants, ses petits maîtres aussi, et les épigones perdus dans les ruines des grands refus.

Cela doit signifier soit que l'effort, les efforts du dernier demi-siècle de peinture en France sont liquidés, les problèmes résolus, la route fermée, soit que l'affaire a tourné court faute d'exécutants.

Ou il ne reste plus rien à faire dans le sens de ces efforts, ou ce qu'il reste à faire ne se fait pas, parce qu'il n'y a personne pour le faire.

Je suggère que la peinture des van Velde est une assurance que l'École de Paris (cf. l'heure de Greenwich) est encore jeune et qu'un bel avenir lui est promis.

Une assurance, une double assurance, car le même deuil les mène loin l'un de l'autre, de deuil de l'objet.

L'histoire de la peinture est l'histoire de ses rapports avec son objet, ceux-ci évoluant, nécessairement, d'abord dans le sens de la largeur, ensuite dans celui de la pénétration. Ce qui renouvelle la peinture, c'est d'abord qu'il y a de plus en plus de choses à peindre, ensuite une façon de les peindre de plus en plus posses-sionnelle. Je n'entends pas par là une première phase toute en épanouissement, suivi d'une seconde toute en concentration, mais seulement deux attitudes liées l'une à l'autre, comme le repos à l'effort. Le frisson primaire de la peinture en prenant conscience de ses limites porte vers les confins de ces limites, le secondaire dans le sens de la profondeur, vers la chose que cache la chose. L'objet de la représentation résiste toujours à la représtentation, soit à cause de ses accidents, soit à cause de sa substance, et d'abord à cause de ses accidents, parce que la connaissance de l'accident précède celle de la substance.

Le premier assaut donné à l'objet saisi, indépendamment de ses qualités, dans son indifférence, son inertie, sa latence, voilà une définition de la peinture moderne qui n'est sans doute pas plus ridicule que les autres. Elle a l'avantage, sans être en rien un jugement de valeur, d'exclure les surréalistes, dont la préoccu-pation, portant uniquement sur des questions de répertoire, reste aussi éloignée de sa grande contemporaine que les Siennois Sassetta et Giovanni di Paolo de l'effort en profondeur de Massaccio et de Castagno. Giovanni di Paolo est un obscurantiste charmant. Elle exclut également ces estimables abstracteurs de quintessence Mondrian, Lissitzky, Malevitsch, Moholy-Nagy. Et elle exprime ce qui est commun à des indépendants aussi divers que Matisse, Bonnard, Villon, Braque, Rouault, Kandinsky, pour ne mentionner qu'eux. Les Christ de Rouault, la nature morte la plus chinoise de Matisse, un conglomérat du Kandinsky de 1943 ou 1944, sont issus du même effort, celui d'exprimer en quoi un clown, une pomme et un carré de rouge ne font qu'un, et du même désarroi, devant la résistance qu'oppose cette unicité à être exprimée. Car ils ne font qu'un en ceci, que ce sont des choses, la chose, la choseté. Il semble absurde de parler, comme faisait Kandinsky, d'une peinture libérée de l'objet. Ce dont la peinture s'est libérée, c'est de l'illusion qu'il existe plus d'un objet de représentation, peut-être même de l'illusion que cet unique objet se laisse représenter.

Si c'est là le dernier état de l'École de Paris, après sa longue poursuite moins de la chose que de sa choseté, moins de l'objet que de la condition d'être, alors on est peut-être en droit de parler d'une crise. Car que reste-t-il de représentable si l'essence de l'objet est de se dérober à la représentation?

Il reste à représenter les conditions de cette dérobade. Elles prendront l'une ou l'autre de deux formes, selon le sujet.

L'un dira: Je ne peux voir l'objet, pour le représenter, parce qu'il est ce qu'il est. L'autre: Je ne peux voir l'objet, pour le représenter, parce que je suis ce que je suis.

Il y a toujours eu ces deux sortes d'artiste, ces deux sortes d'empêchement, l'empêchement-objet et l'empêchement-oeil. Mais ces empêchements, on en tenait compte. Il y avait accommodation. Ils ne faisaient pas partie de la représentation, ou à peine. Ici ils en font partie. On dirait la plus grande partie. Est peint ce qui empêche de peindre.

Geer van Velde est un artiste de la première sorte (à mon chancelant avis), Bram van Velde de la seconde.

Leur peinture est l'analyse d'un état de privation, analyse empruntant chez l'un les termes du dehors, la lumière et le vide, chez l'autre ceux du dedans, l'obscurité, le plein, la phosphorescence.

La résolution s'obtient chez l'un par l'abandon du poids, de la densité, de la solidité, par un déchirement de tout ce qui gâche l'espace, arrête la lumière, par l'engloutissement du dehors sous les conditions du dehors. Chez l'autre parmi les masses inébranlables d'un être écarté, enfermé et rentré pour toujours en lui-même, sans traces, sans air, cyclopéen, aux brefs éclairs, aux couleurs du spectre du noir.

Un dévoilement sans fin, voile derrière voile, plan sur plan de transparences imparfaites, un dévoilement vers l'indévoilable, le rien, la chose à nouveau. Et l'ensevelissement dans l'unique, dans un lieu d'impénétrables proximités, cellule peinte sur la pierre de la cellule, art d'incarcération.

Voilà ce à quoi il faut s'attendre quand on se laisse couillonner à écrire sur la peinture. A moins d'être un critique d'art.

La peinture des van Velde sort, libre de tout souci critique, d'une peinture de critique et de refus, refus d'accepter comme donné le vieux rapport sujet-objet. Il est évident que toute oeuvre d'art est un rajustement de ce rapport, mais sans en être une critique dans le sens où le meilleur de la peinture moderne en est une critique qui dans ses dernières manifestations ressemble fort à celle qu'on adresse, avec un bâton, aux lenteurs de l'âne mort.

A partir de ce moment il reste trois chemins que la peinture peut prendre. Le chemin du retour à vieille naïveté, à travers l'hiver de son abandon, le chemin des repentis. Puis le chemin qui n'en est plus un, mais une dernière tentative de vivre sur le pays conquis. Et enfin le chemin en avant d'une peinture qui se soucie aussi peu d'une convention périmée que des hiératismes et préciosités des enquêtes superflues, peinture d'acceptation, entrevoyant dans l'absence de rapport et dans l'absence d'objet le nouveau rapport et le nouvel objet, chemin qui bifurque déjà, dans les travaux de Bram et de Geer van Velde.

4. Three Dialogues

I
Tal Coat

B. — Total object, complete with missing parts, instead of partial object. Question of degree.

D. — More. The tyranny of the discreet overthrown. The world a flux of movements partaking of living time, that of effort, creation, liberation, the painting, the painter. The fleeting instant of sensation given back, given forth, with context of the continuum it nourished.

B. — In any case a thrusting towards a more adequate expression of natural experience, as revealed to the vigilant coenaesthesia. Whether achieved through submission or through mastery, the result is a gain in nature.

D. — But that which this painter discovers, orders, transmits, is not in nature. What relation between one of these paintings and a landscape seen at a certain age, a certain season, a certain hour? Are we not on a quite different plane?

B. — By nature I mean here, like the naivest realist, a composite of perceiver and perceived, not a datum, an experience. All I wish to suggest is that the tendency and accomplishment of this painting are fundamentally those of previous painting, straining to enlarge the statement of a compromise.

D. — You neglect the immense difference between the significance of perception for Tal Coat and its significance for the great majority of his predecessors, apprehending as artists with the same utilitarian servility as in a traffic jam and improving the result with a lick of Euclidian geometry. The global perception of Tal Coat is disinterested, committed neither to truth nor to beauty, twin tyrannies of nature. I can see the compromise of past painting, but not that which you deplore in the Matisse of a certain period and in the Tal Coat of today.

B. — I do not deplore. I agree that the Matisse in question, as well as the Franciscan orgies of Tal Coat, have prodigious value, but a value cognate with those already accumulated. What we have to consider in the case of Italian painters is not that they surveyed the world with the eyes of building contractors, a mere means like any other, but that they never stirred from the field of the possible, however much they may have enlarged it. The only thing disturbed by the revolutionaries Matisse and Tal Coat is a certain order on the plane of the feasible.

D. — What other plane can there be for the maker?

B. — Logically none. Yet I speak of an art turning from it in disgust, weary of its puny exploits, weary of pretending to be able, of being able, of doing a little better the same old thing, of going a little further along a dreary road.

D. — And preferring what?

B. — The expression that there is nothing to express, nothing with which to express, nothing from which to express, no power to express, no desire to express, together with the obligation to express.

D. — But that is a violently extreme and personal point of view, of no help to us in the matter of Tal Coat.

B.—

D. — Perhaps that is enough for today.

II
Masson

B. — In search of the difficulty rather than in its clutch. The disquiet of him who lacks an adversary.

D. — That is perhaps why he speaks so often nowadays of painting the void, 'in fear and trembling'. His concern was at one time with the creation of a mythology; then with man, not simply in the universe, but in society; and now . . . 'inner emptiness, the prime condition, according to Chinese esthetics, of the act of painting'. It would thus seem, in effect, that Masson suffers more keenly than any living painter from the need to come to rest, i.e. to establish the data of the problem to be solved, the Problem at last.

B. — Though little familiar with the problems he has set himself in the past and which, by the mere fact of their solubility or for any other reason, have lost for him their legitimacy, I feel their presence not far behind these canvases veiled in consternation, and the scars of a competence that must be most painful to him. Two old maladies that should no doubt be considered separately: the malady of wanting to know what to do and the malady of wanting to be able to do it.

D. — But Masson's declared purpose is now to reduce these maladies, as you call them, to nothing. He aspires to be rid of the servitude of space, that his eye may 'frolic among the focusless fields, tumultuous with incessant creation'. At the same time he demands the rehabilitation of the 'vaporous'. This may seem strange in one more fitted by temperament for fire than for damp. You of course will reply that it is the same thing as before, the same reaching towards succour from without. Opaque or transparent, the object remains sovereign. But how can Masson be expected to paint the void?

B. — He is not. What is the good of passing from one untenable position to another, of seeking justification always on the same plane? Here is an artist who seems literally skewered on the ferocious dilemma of expression. Yet he continues to wriggle. The void he speaks of is perhaps simply the obliteration of an unbearable presence, unbearable because neither to be wooed nor to be stormed. If this anguish of helplessness is never stated as such, on its own merits and for its own sake, though perhaps very occasionally admitted as spice to the 'exploit' it jeopardized, the reason is doubtless, among others, that it seems to contain in itself the impossibility of statement. Again an exquisitely logical attitude. In any case, it is hardly to be confused with the void.

D. — Masson speaks much of transparency — 'openings, circulations, communications, unknown penetrations' — where he may frolic at his ease, in freedom. Without renouncing the objects, loathsome or delicious, that are our daily bread and wine and poison, he seeks to break through their partitions to that continuity of being which is absent from the ordinary experience of living. In this he approaches Matisse (of the first period needless to say) and Tal Coat, but with this notable difference, that Masson has to contend with his own technical gifts, which have the richness, the precision, the density and balance of the high classical manner. Or perhaps I should say rather its spirit, for he has shown himself capable, as occasion required, of great technical variety.

B. — What you say certainly throws light on the dramatic predicament of this artist. Allow me to note his concern with the amenities of ease and freedom. *The stars are undoubtedly superb*, as Freud remarked on reading Kant's cosmological proof of the existence of God. With such preoccupations it seems to me impossible that he should ever do anything different from that which the best, including himself, have done already. It is perhaps an impertinence to suggest that he wishes to. His so extremely intelligent remarks on space breathe the same possessiveness as the notebooks of Leonardo who, when he speaks of *disfazione*, knows that for him not one fragment will be lost. So forgive me if I relapse, as when we spoke of the so different Tal Coat, into my dream of an art unresentful of its insuperable indigence and too proud for the farce of giving and receiving.

D. — Masson himself, having remarked that western perspective is no more than a series of traps for the capture of objects, declares that their possession does not interest him. He congratulates Bonnard for having, in his last works, 'gone beyond possessive space in every shape and form, far from surveys and bounds, to the point where all possession is dissolved.' I agree that there is a long cry from Bonnard to that impoverished painting, 'authentically fruitless, incapable of any image whatsoever', to which you aspire, and towards which too, who knows, unconsciously perhaps, Masson tends. But must we really deplore the painting that admits 'the things and creatures of spring, resplendent with desire and affirmation, ephemeral no doubt, but immortally reiterant', not in order to benefit by them, not in order to enjoy them, but in order that what is tolerable and radiant in the world may continue? Are we really to deplore the painting that is a

141

rallying, among the things of time that pass and hurry us away, towards a time that endures and gives increase?

B. — *(Exit weeping.)*

III
Bram van Velde

B. — Frenchman, fire first.

D. — Speaking of Tal Coat and Masson you invoked an art of a different order, not only from theirs, but from any achieved up to date. Am I right in thinking that you had van Velde in mind when making this sweeping distinction?

B. — Yes. I think he is the first to accept a certain situation and to consent to a certain act.

D. — Would it be too much to ask you to state again, as simply as possible, the situation and act that you conceive to be his?

B. — The situation is that of him who is helpless, cannot act, in the event cannot paint, since he is obliged to paint. The act is of him who, helpless, unable to act, acts, in the event paints, since he is obliged to paint.

D. — Why is he obliged to paint?

B. — I don't know.

D. — Why is he helpless to paint?

B. — Because there is nothing to paint and nothing to paint with.

D. — And the result, you say, is art of a new order?

B. — Among those whom we call great artists, I can think of none whose concern was not predominantly with his expressive possibilities, those of his vehicle, those of humanity. The assumption underlying all painting is that the domain of the maker is the domain of the feasible. The much to express, the little to express, the ability to express much, the ability to express little, merge in the common anxiety to express as much as possible, or as truly as possible, or as finely as possible, to the best of one's ability. What—

D. — One moment. Are you suggesting that the painting of van Velde is inexpressive?

B. — *(A fortnight later)* Yes.

D. — You realize the absurdity of what you advance?

B. — I hope I do.

D. — What you say amounts to this: the form of expression known as painting, since for obscure reasons we are obliged to speak of painting, has had to wait for van Velde to be rid of the misapprehension under which it had laboured so long and so bravely, namely, that its function was to express, by means of paint.

B. — Others have felt that art is not necessarily expression. But the numerous attempts made to make painting independent of its occasion have only succeeded in enlarging its repertory. I suggest that ven Velde is the first whose painting is bereft, rid if you prefer, of occasion in every shape and form, ideal as well as material, and the first whose hands have not been tied by the certitude that expression is an impossible act.

D. — But might it not be suggested, even by one tolerant of this fantastic theory, that the occasion of his painting is his predicament, and that it is expressive of the impossibility to express?

B. — No more ingenious method could be devised for restoring him, safe and sound, to the bosom of Saint Luke. But let us for once, be foolish enough not to turn tail. All have turned wisely tail, before the ultimate penury, back to the mere misery where destitute virtuous mothers may steal stale bread for their starving brats. There is more than a difference of degree between being short, short of the world, short of self, and being without these esteemed commodities. The one is a predicament, the other not.

D. — But you have already spoken of the predicament of van Velde.

B. — I should not have done so.

D. — You prefer the purer view that here at last is a painter who does not paint, does not pretend to paint. Come, come, my dear fellow, make some kind of connected statement and then go away.

B. — Would it not be enough if I simply went away?

D. — No. You have begun. Finish. Begin again and go on until you have finished. Then go away. Try and bear in mind that the subject under discussion is not yourself, not the Sufist Al-Haqq, but a particular Dutchman by name van Velde, hitherto erroneously referred to as an *artiste peintre*.

B. — How would it be if I first said what I am pleased to fancy he is, fancy he does, and then that it is more than likely that he is and does quite otherwise? Would not that be an excellent issue out of all our afflictions? He happy, you happy, I happy, all three bubbling over with happiness.

D. — Do as you please. But get it over.

B. — There are many ways in which the thing I am trying in vain to say may be tried in vain to be said. I have experimented, as you know, both in public and in private, under duress, through faintness of heart, through weakness of mind, with two or three hundred. The pathetic antithesis possession-poverty was perhaps not the most tedious. But we begin to weary of it, do we not? The realization that art has always been bourgeois, thugh it may dull our pain before the achievements of the socially progressive, is finally of scant interest. The analysis of the relation between the artist and his occasion, a relation always regarded as indispensable, does not seem to have been very productive either, the reason being perhaps that it lost its way in disquisitions on the nature of occasion. It is obvious that for the artist obsessed with his expressive vocation, anything and everything is doomed to become occasion, including, as is apparently to some extent the case with Masson, the pursuit of occasion, and the every man his own wife experiments of the spiritual Kandinsky. No painting is more replete than Mondrian's. But if the occasion appears as an unstable term of relation, the artist, who is the other term, is hardly less so, thanks to his warren of modes and attitudes. The objections to this dualist view of the creative process are unconvincing. Two things are established, however precariously: the aliment, from fruits on plates to low mathematics and self-commiseration, and its manner of dispatch. All that should concern us is the acute and increasing anxiety of the relation itself, as though shadowed more and more darkly by a sense of invalidity, of inadequacy, of existence at the expense of all that it excludes, all that it blinds to. The history of painting, here we go again, is the history of its attempts to escape from this sense of failure, by means of more authentic, more ample, less exclusive relations between representer and representee, in a kind of tropism towards a light as to the nature of which the best opinions continue to vary, and with a kind of Pythagorean terror, as though the irrationality of pi were an offence against the deity, not to mention his creature. My case, since I am in the dock, is that van Velde is the first to desist from this estheticized automatism, the first to admit that to be an artist is to fail, as no other dare fail, that failure is his world and the shrink from it desertion, art and craft, good housekeeping, living. No, no, allow me to expire. I know that all that is required now, in order to bring even this horrible matter to an acceptable conclusion, is to make of this submission, this admission, this fidelity to failure, a new occasion, a new term of relation, and of the act which, unable to act, obliged to act, he makes, an expressive act, even if only of itself, of its impossibility, of its obligation. I know that my inability to do so places myself, and perhaps an innocent, in what I think is still called an unenviable situation, familiar to psychiatrists. For what is this coloured plane, that was not there before. I don't know what it is, having never seen anything like it before. It seems to have nothing to do with art, in any case, if my memories of art are correct. *(Prepares to go.)*

D. — Are you not forgetting something?

B. — Surely that is enough?

D. — I understood your number was to have two parts. The first was to consist in your saying what you — er — thought. This I am prepared to believe you have done. The second —

B. — *(Remembering, warmly)* Yes, yes, I am mistaken, I am mistaken.

5. Henri Hayden, homme-peintre

On me demande des mots, à moi qui n'en ai plus, plus guère, sur une chose qui les récuse. Exécutons-nous, exécutons-la.

Gautama, avant qu'ils vinssent à lui manquer, disait qu'on se trompe en affirmant que le moi existe, mais qu'en affirmant qu'il n'existe pas on ne se trompe pas moins.

Il s'entend dans les toiles de Hayden, loin derrière leur patient silence, comme l'écho de cette folle sagesse et, tout bas, de son corollaire, à savoir que pour le reste il ne peut qu'en être de même.

Présence à peine de celui qui fait, présence à peine de ce qui est fait. Oeuvre impersonnelle, oeuvre irréelle. C'est une chose des plus curieuses que ce double effacement. Et d'une bien hautaine inactualité. Elle n'est pas au bout de ses beaux jours, la crise sujet-objet. Mais c'est à part et au profit l'un de l'autre que nous avons l'habitude de les voir défaillir, ce clown et son gugusse. Alors qu'ici, confondus dans une même inconsistance, ils se désistent de concert.

Pas trace des grandes périclitations, des remises debout sous la trique de la raison, des exploits du tempérament exclusif, des quintessentialismes à froid, de tous les recours et subterfuges d'une peinture en perte de références et qui ne visent plus au fond à faire plus beau, aussi beau, autrement beau, mais tout bonnement à sauver un rapport, un écart, un couple quelque diminués qu'en soient les composants, le moi dans ses possibilités d'agir, de recevoir, le reste dans ses docilités de donnée. Pas trace de surenchère, ni dans l'outrance ni dans la carence. Mais l'acceptation, aussi peu satisfaite qu'amère, de tout ce qu'a d'insubstantiel et d'infime, comme entre ombres, le choc dont sort l'oeuvre.

Ceci à condition, devant ces paysages et natures mortes, de sentir (plutôt que de voir) combien est fragile leur touchante assurance de formes familières et tout l'équivoque de ces arbres qui abandonnent aussitôt partis, de ces fruits qu'on dirait victimes d'une erreur de distribution. Il s'en dégage un humour à peine perciptible, à peine triste, comme de celui qui de loin se prête une dernière fois aux jeux d'un fabuleux cher et révolu, un *risolino* à l'Arioste. Tout est reconnaissable, mais à s'y méconnaître. Etrange ordre des choses, fait d'ordre en mal de choses, de choses en mal d'ordre.

La hantise et en même temps le refus du peu, c'est peut-être à cela qu'un jour on finira par reconnaître notre cher vieux bon temps. De ce peu d'où l'on se précipite, comme de la pire des malédictions, vers les prestiges du tout et du rien. D'inoubliables artifices l'attesteront. Mais qu'il se soit trouvé, tranquillement sans espoir au milieu de tant de ruades, un peintre pour ne pas fuir, pour endurer d'un soi tel quel et d'une nature imprenable les mirages, les intermittences et les dérisoires échanges et pour en soutirer une oeuvre, à la famélique mesure de l'homme et de son bouillon de culture Chartier, c'est ce dont pour ma part, devant les toiles de Henri Hayden, je ne m'étais pas assez étonné, ni avec de fraternelle affection. Le voilà, cela au moins, chose faite.

6. Hommage à Jack B. Yeats

Ce qu'a d'incomparable cette grande oeuvre solitaire est son insistance à renvoyer au plus secret de l'esprit qui la soulève et à ne se laisser éclairer qu'au jour de celui-ci.

Da là cette étrangeté sans exemple et que laissent entière les habituels recours aux patrimoines, national et autres.

Quoi de moins féerique que cette prestigieuse facture comme soufflée par la chose à faire, et par son urgence propre?

Quant aux repondants qu'on a bien fini par lui dénicher, Ensor et Munch en tête, le moins qu'on puisse en dire est qu'ils ne nous sont pas d'un grand secours.

L'artiste qui joue son être est de nulle part. Et il n'a pas de frères.

Broder alors? Sur ces images éperdument immédiates il n'y a ni place, ni temps, pour les exploits rassurants. Sur cette violence de besoin qui non seulement des déchaîne, mais les bouleverse jusqu'au delà de leur horizons. Sur ce grand réel intérieur où fantômes morts et vivants, nature et vide, tout ce qui n'a de cesse et tout ce qui ne sera jamais, s'intègrent en une seule évidence et pour une seule déposition.

Enfin sur cette suprême maîtrise qui se soumet à l'immaîtrisable, et tremble.

Non.

S'incliner simplement, émerveillé.

Homage to Jack B. Yeats

High solitary art uniquely self-pervaded, one with its wellhead in a hiddenmost of spirit, not to be clarified in any other light.

Strangeness so entire as even to withstand the stock assimilations to holy patrimony, national and other.

What less celt than this incomparable hand shaken by the aim it sets itself or by its own urgency?

As for the sureties kindly unearthed in his favour, Ensor and Munch to the fore, the least one can say is that they are no great help.

The artist who stakes his being is from nowhere, has no kith.

Gloss? In images of such breathless immediacy as these there is no occasion, no time given, no room left, for the lenitive of comment. None in this impetus of need that scatters them loose to the beyonds of vision. None in this great inner real where phantoms quick and dead, nature and void, all that ever and that never will be, join in a single evidence for a single testimony. None in this final mastery which submits in trembling to the unmasterable.

No.

Merely bow in wonder.

7. Henri Hayden

Cinquante années de peinture d'une indépendance et d'une gravité exemplaires, c'est ce que vient de nous offrir la rétrospective Hayden au très beau Musée des Beaux-Arts de Lyon.

De ce grand peinture solitaire nous avons l'honneur de présenter aujourd'hui un ensemble de gouaches récentes. Leur beauté est le fait d'un artiste qui a su, toute sa vie et comme peu d'autres, résister aux deux grandes tentations, celle du réel et celle du mensonge.

8. Bram van Velde

'La vie — écrit Pierre Schneider, dans son bel essai sur Corbière
— est une faute d'orthographe dans le texte de la mort.' Il en est
heureusement de plus sérieuses. Celles dont voici les laves.
Balayés les repentirs. Peinture de vie et de mort. Amateurs de
natron, abstenez.

9. Pour Avigdor Arikha

Siège remis devant le dehors imprenable. Fièvre oeil-main dans la soif du non-soi. Oeil par la main sans cesse changé à l'instant même où sans cesse il la change. Regard ne s'arrachant à l'invisible que pour s'asséner sur l'infaisable et retour éclair. Trêve à la navette et traces de ce que c'est que d'être et d'être devant. Traces profondes.

For Avigdor Arikha

Siege laid again to the impregnable without. Eye and hand fevering after the unself. By the hand it unceasingly changes the eye unceasingly changed. Back and forth the gaze beating against unseeable and unmakable. Truce for a space and the marks of what it is to be and be in face of. Those deep marks to show.

Part IV

Human Wishes

Human Wishes

ACT 1

A room in Bolt Court. Wednesday, April 14th, 1781. Evening.

Mrs Williams *(meditating).*
Mrs Desmoulins *(knitting).*
Miss Carmichael *(reading).*
The cat Hodge *(sleeping — if possible).*

Mrs D.   He is late.

Silence.

Mrs D.   God grant all is well.

Silence.

Mrs D.   Puss puss puss puss puss.

Silence.

Mrs W.   What are you reading, young woman?

Miss C.   A book, Madam.

Mrs W.   Ha!

Silence.

Mrs D.   Hodge is a very fine cat, a very fine cat indeed.

Silence.

Mrs D.   For his age, an uncommonly fine cat in all respects.
When Hodge was a younger cat, I well remember —

Mrs W.   You are knotting, Madam, I perceive.

Mrs D.   That is so, Madam.

Mrs W.   What?

Mrs D.   I am knotting, my dear Madam, a mitten.

Mrs W.   Ha!

Mrs D.   The second of a pair.

Silence.

Mrs W.   What book, young woman?

Silence.

Mrs W.   *(loudly).* I say, WHAT BOOK?

Miss C.   Upon my soul, Madam, your perceptions are very fine, very fine indeed, uncommonly fine in all respects.

Mrs W.   I may be old, I may be blind, halt and maim, I may be dying of a pituitous defluxion, but my hearing is unimpaired.

Miss C.   And your colloquial powers.

Mrs D.   Dying of a what, my dear Madam?

Mrs W.   And while I continue to live, or rather to respire, I hope I shall never submit to be insulted by sluts, slovens, upstarts, parasites and intruders.

Mrs D.   Come, come, my dear lady.

Mrs W.   Knot on, Madam, knot on, or endeavour to talk like a sensible woman.

Mrs D.   You wish to provoke me, Madam, but I am not provoked. The peevishness of decay is not provoking.

Miss C.   Insupportable hag.

Mrs D.   *(rising).* That is not the language of a gentlewoman, Miss Carmichael.

Miss C.   *(rising).* I have not the advantage, Madam, of being the relict of a writing-master.

Mrs W.   *(striking the floor with her stick).* Be seated; and let your scurrility be the recumbent scurrility of polite society.

Miss C.   Nor the daughter of a Welsh mechanic.

Mrs D.   Of whom you are the relict, Miss Carmichael, or of how many, I prefer not to enquire.

Mrs W.   Were I not loath, Madam, to abase myself to your syntax, I could add: or of whom the daughter, or of how many.

Miss C.   *(laughs heartily, sits down and resumes her book).*

Mrs W.   Is the jest yours, Madam, or it is mine?

Mrs D.   To be called a loose woman would not move me to mirth, for my part, I believe. *(Sits down).*

Mrs W.   And to be called the daughter of a loose woman, would that move you to mirth, Madam, for your part, do you suppose?

Mrs D.   It would not, Madam, I believe.

-Mrs W.   But what would move you, Madam, to mirth, do you suppose, for your part?

Mrs D.   To mirth, Madam, for my part, I am with difficulty moved, I believe.

Silence.

Mrs W.   Madam, for mirth, for my part,
I never had the heart;
Madam, for my part, to mirth
I have not been moved since birth.

Silence.

Mrs W.   Please to take it down. I repeat. *(Repeats).*

Silence.

Mrs W.   Is it down?

Miss C.   It is, Madam. In what will not dry black and what was never white.

Mrs W.   Give it to me here in my hand.

Miss C.   *(rises, takes a blank sheet off the table, hands it to Mrs. W. and returns to her seat).*

Mrs W.   (*fingering the sheet tenderly*). I did not hear the scratch of the quill.

Miss C.   I write very quiet.

Mrs W.   I do not feel the trace of the ink.

Miss C.   I write very fine. Very quiet, I write, and very fine.

Silence.

Mrs W.   Mrs Desmoulins.

Mrs D.   Madam.

Mrs W.   You have ceased to knot, I perceive.

Mrs D.   That is so, Madam.

Silence.

Mrs W.   Mrs Desmoulins.

Mrs D.   What is it, Madam?

Mrs W.   You say you are not merry. Very well. But who is merry in this house? You would not call me merry, Madam, I suppose?

Mrs D.   No, Madam, you are not what I would call merry.

Mrs W.   And Frank, Madam, would you call Frank merry?

Mrs D.   No, Madam, I would not.

Miss C.   Except when drunk.

Mrs D.   The gross hilarity of ebriety is not merriment, Miss Carmichael, to my mind.

Mrs W.   And Levett, Madam, would you call Levett merry?

Mrs D.   I would not call Levett anything, Madam.

Miss C.   Not even when drunk.

Mrs W.   And poor Poll here, Madam, is poor Poll here what you would call merry?

Mrs D.   She was taken into the house to be merry.

Mrs W.   I do not ask why she was taken into the house. I ask is she merry or is she not merry.

Miss C.   I was merry once, I think.

Mrs W.   *(loudly)*. What is it to me, Miss, that you were merry once? Are you merry, or are you not merry, NOW?

Mrs D.   She was taken in to enliven the house. I do not feel myself enlivened, for my part.

Mrs W.   What you feel, Madam, and what you do not feel, is of little consequence.

Mrs D.   I am aware of that, Madam.

Mrs W.   I am not merry, you are not merry, Frank is not merry —

Miss C.   Except when drunk.

Mrs W.   Silence! Levett is not merry. Who remains?

Miss C.   The cat.

Mrs W.   *(striking the floor with her stick)*. Silence!

Silence.

Mrs W.   The cat does *not* remain. The cat does not enter into the question. The cat *cannot* be merry.

Silence.

Mrs W.   I ask, who remains?

Silence.

Mrs W.   *(loudly)*. I ask, who remains, who might be merry?

Mrs D.   Who was taken into the house to be merry.

Mrs W.   *(striking the floor with her stick)*. Silence!

Silence.

Mrs W.   I ask, who remains who might be merry, and I answer *(pointing her stick at Miss Carmichael)*, she remains.

Silence.

Mrs W.   Is she merry?

Silence.

Mrs W.   *(at the top of her voice).* IS SHE MERRY?

Miss C.   *(softly).* She is not.

Silence.

Mrs W.   *(softly).* Nobody in this house is merry.

Mrs D.   I hope you are satisfied, Madam.

Silence.

Miss C.   And the doctor, is the doctor. . . .

Silence.

Mrs D.   He is late.

Silence.

Mrs D.   God grant all is well.

Enter LEVETT, *slightly, respectably, even reluctantly drunk, in great coat and hat, which he does not remove, carrying a small black bag. He advances unsteadily into the room & stands peering at the company. Ignored ostentatiously by Mrs D. (knitting), Miss Carmichael (reading), Mrs W. (meditating), he remains a little standing as though lost in thought, then suddenly emits a single hiccup of such force that he is almost thrown off his feet. Startled from her knitting Mrs D., from her book Miss C., from her stage meditation Mrs W., survey him with indignation. L. remains standing a little longer, absorbed & motionless, then on a wide tack returns cautiously to the door, which he does not close behind him. His unsteady footsteps are heard on the stairs. Between the three women exchange of looks. Gestures of disgust. Mouths opened and shut. Finally they resume their occupations.*

Mrs W.   Words fail us.

Mrs D.   Now this is where a writer for the stage would have us speak no doubt.

Mrs W.   He would have us explain Levett.

Mrs D.   To the public.

Mrs W. The ignorant public.

Mrs D. To the gallery.

Mrs W. To the pit.

Miss C. To the boxes.

Mrs W. Mr Murphy.

Mrs D. Mr Kelly.

Miss C. Mr Goldsmith.

Mrs D. Let us not speak unkindly of the departed.

Miss C. The departed?

Mrs D. Can you be unaware, Miss, that the dear doctor's debt to nature —

Mrs W. Not a very large one.

Mrs D. That the dear doctor's debt to nature is discharged these seven years.

Mrs W. More.

Mrs D. Seven years to-day, Madam, almost to the hour, neither more nor less.

Miss C. His debt to nature?

Mrs W. She means the wretched man is dead.

Miss C. Dead!

Mrs W. Dead. D-E-A-D. Expired. Like the late Queen Anne and the Rev. Edward ——.

Miss C. Well I am heartily sorry indeed to hear that.

Mrs W. So was I, Miss, heartily sorry indeed to hear it, at the time, being of the opinion, as I still am, that before paying his debt to nature he might have paid his debt to me. Seven shillings and sixpence, extorted on the contemptible security of his *Animated Nature*. He asked for a guinea.

Mrs D. There are many, Madam, more sorely disappointed,

willing to forget the frailties of a life long since trans-
ported to that undiscovered country from whose —

Mrs W.   *(striking the floor with her stick)*. None of your Shakespeare
to me, Madam. The fellow may be in Abraham's
bosom for aught I know or care, I still say he ought to
be in Newgate.

Mrs D.   *(sighs and goes back to her knitting)*.

Mrs W.   I am dead enough myself, I hope, not to feel any great
respect for those that are so entirely.

Silence.

Mrs W.   Also I should very much like to know, Madam, if the
power of speech has not deserted you, for what reason
it is improper in poor Poll here to mention the 'dear
doctor', and proper in you to pronounce the sacred
name of that drunken staymaker Hugh Kelly, dead and
damned these five years.

Mrs D.   You are mistaken, Madam.

Mrs W.   In what am I mistaken?

Mrs D.   In saying that Mr Kelly is no longer with us. It is
impossible that the creator of *False Delicacy* should have
been laid to rest and the fact not come to my notice.

Mrs w.   Your notice! After fifty years of dropped stitches, pious
exertions and charity-brats, you still speak of your
notice.

Mrs D.   *(scorns to reply)*.

Mrs W.   And your 'laid to rest'! Laid to rest in lakes of boiling
small-beer, with his Dublin publican papa, that's
where he's laid to rest, your stayless, playless, briefless,
drunken party-scribbler.

Mrs D.   Miss Carmichael, would you have the great goodness to
close the door.

Miss C.   I would not, Madam.

Mrs W.   *(at the top of her voice)*. KELLY IS DEAD, MADAM.

Mrs D.   *(rising).* I have nothing more to say, Madam, but that you are mistaken, most offensively mistaken. *(Exit, banging door behind her).*

Enter Mrs D. She speaks from the threshold.

Mrs D.   Mr Kelly is alive and, I trust, drawing his pension without encumbrance. Mr Kelly may be poorly, but he is alive, and, I pray God, drawing his pension without encumbrance. *(Exit, banging door.)*

Enter Mrs D. as before.

Mrs D.   Should however Mr Kelly, by some extraordinary haphazard, be no longer alive —

Mrs W.   Nor drawing his pension without encumberland.

Mrs D.   And the fact not have come to my notice, I . . . I . . . *(Weeps).*

Mrs D.   I shall regret it bitterly . . . bitterly . . . *(Exit, closing door softly).*

Silence.

Mrs W.   Forgive me. I was musing.

Silence.

Mrs W.   I was musing as to whether what she . . . what the . . . *(Breaks off. Strikes floor with stick).* Pest!

Silence.

Mrs W.   I was musing thus: is what she bitterly regrets, what already it may be she . . . *(Breaks off. Strikes floor with stick).* PEST!

Silence.

Mrs W.   *(in a strong decided tone).* What will the woman bitterly regret, if she does not do so already, the death of Kelly or the fact not having come to her notice.

Silence.

Mrs W.   There is a notice of the mind and there is a notice of the heart. The first is nothing. And the heart is cold.

Silence.

Mrs W.   *(now evidently talking to herself).* For years, for how many years every day, dead, whose name I had known, whose face I had seen, whose voice I had heard, whose hand I had held, whose — but it is idle to continue. Yesterday, in the flower of her age, Mrs Winterbotham, the greengrocer of the Garden; Monday, Mr Pott of the Fleet; Sunday, in great pain, in his home in Islington, after a lingering illness, surrounded by his family, the Very Reverend William Walter Okey, Litt.D., LL.D; Saturday, at Bath, suddenly, Miss Tout; Friday, — but it is idle to continue. I know —

Miss C.   And to-day, Madam?

Mrs W.   *(with a start).* I beg your pardon?

Miss C.   And to-day, Madam.

Mrs W.   To-day is not yet over, Miss Carmichael.

Silence.

Mrs W.   I know they are dead, their deaths are come to the notice of my mind.

Silence.

Mrs W.   When my father, Mr Zachariah Williams, died, on the 12th of June, seventeen hundred and fifty-five (old time), at twelve at night, in his eighty third year, after an illness of eight months, in full possession of his mental faculties, I knew at once he was dead. He died, and at once I knew he was dead. I wept, because one weeps, when one's father dies. I remember turning, that morning, with tears in my eyes, whose vigour even then was beginning to abate, the pages of his pamphlet: *An Account of an Attempt to Ascertain the Longitude at Sea: with a Table of the Variations at the most Remarkable Cities in Europe.*

Silence.

Mrs W.   But it did not come to the notice of my heart until the Christmas following.

Silence.

Miss C. 'Death meets us everywhere, and is procured by every instrument and in all chances, and enters in at many doors; by violence —'

Mrs W. What twaddle is this, Miss Carmichael?

Miss C. I am reading from my book, Madam.

Mrs W. I did not suppose you were inventing it.

Miss C. 'By violence and secret influence; by the aspect of a star and the stink of a mist —'

Mrs W. The stink of a mist?

Miss C. Yes, Madam, the stink of a mist.

Mrs W. Continue, continue.

Miss C. 'Of a mist; by the emissions of a cloud and the meeting of a vapour; by the fall of a chariot and the stumbling at a stone; by a full meal or an empty stomach; by watching at the wine or by watching at prayers; by the sun or the moon; by a heat or a cold; by sleepless nights or sleeping days; by water frozen or water thawed; by a hair or a raisin —'

Mrs W. A hair or a raisin?*

Miss C. Yes, Madam, a hair or a raisin.

Mrs W. How do you suppose death enters in by a hair, Miss Carmichael?

Miss C. Perhaps a horse-hair is meant, Madam.

Mrs W. Perhaps so indeed. I know if death would be content to enter into me by a horse-hair, or by any other manner of hair for that matter, I should be very much obliged to him.

Miss C. 'By a hair or a raisin; by violent exertion or by sitting still; by severity or dissolution; by God's mercy or

---

*Beckett's fair copy ends here, but the holograph continues to 'Taylor.'

God's anger; by everything in Providence and everything in manners, by everything in nature and everything in chance.'

Silence.

Mrs W.   Brown for a guinea.

Miss Carmichael rises.

Mrs W.   I say: Brown for a guinea.

Miss C.   I hear you, Madam.

Mrs W.   Then answer me. Is it Brown or is it not Brown?

Miss C.   Brown or Black, Madam, it is all one to me.

Mrs W.   Is it possible she reads and does not know what she reads.

Miss C.   I read so little, Madam, it is all one to me.

Mrs W.   Turn to the title page, my child, and tell me is it Brown.

Miss C.   *(turning to the title page).* Taylor.

Notes

Part I

Dante . . . Bruno . Vico . . Joyce. Beckett's first non-juvenile publication appeared in 1929 in both book (*Our Exagmination Round his Factification for Incamination of Work in Progress*: Paris, Shakespeare and Company) and periodical (*transition* 16–17). Those indispensable Beckett bibliographers, Federman and Fletcher, quote Beckett on the idiosyncratic punctuation of his title: 'From Dante to Bruno is a jump of about three centuries, from Bruno to Vico about one, and from Vico to Joyce about two.' The subject was suggested by Joyce, but Beckett dispensed the proportions — almost half the essay expounding Vico, a bare nod offered to Bruno, and parallel admiration accorded to Dante and Joyce.

Le Concentrisme. This untitled, unpublished manuscript was long believed missing, and it is now on permanent loan to the Beckett Collection of the University of Reading Library. The typescript is undated, but 1930 seems probable, after Beckett's two Parisian years as *lecteur* at the Ecole Normale Supérieure, which considers itself very superior indeed. Normalian hoaxes are not infrequent, and in that spirit Beckett invents Jean du Chas, who shares his own birthdate, April 13, 1906, as well as his affection for darkness, solitude, negation, and crisp epigrams. The famous ennui of *Waiting for Godot* is predicted comically in the Chasien motto: 'Va t'embêter ailleurs' which Beckett has translated (in a personal letter): 'Feck off.' Beneath the brittle surface of *Le Concentrisme*, Beckett nevertheless gropes towards an esthetic. (The sterile academic attitude links the Jean du Chas of *Concentrisme* to a minor character of the same name in Beckett's 1932 *Dream of Fair to Middling Women.* Alive and sociable, the latter du Chas is a Parisian in Dublin.)

Excerpts from *Dream of Fair to Middling Women.* Beckett's first novel exists in typescript in the Baker Memorial Library of Dartmouth College, New Hampshire. Written in a Paris hotel in 1932, *Dream* follows its reasonably awake protagonist Belacqua from Dublin to Vienna, Paris, and back to Dublin. Beckett's first sustained fictional effort harbors his own esthetic cogitations. The *Dream's* anonymous, self-flaunting narrator enunciates the first group of excerpts, *a* through *e*. A pseudo-Chinese tale implies that musicians have an easier task than writers in controlling their material within a closed system, and an astral rhapsody hails an irrational art. The narrator complains about the protagonist Belacqua who may 'drop a book'; he in turn meditates on a transparent style. In a dialogue with his Vienna love's father (Irish in spite of his mock-Chinese title of Mandarin), Belacqua espouses incoherent art. Above all, Belacqua indulges in an interior monologue about art, which forecasts Beckett's French fiction, with its 'punctuation of dehiscence'.

German Letter of 1937. Dated July 9, 1937, this unusually explicit critical statement is found in typescript in the Baker Memorial Library of Dartmouth College. Axel Kaun, an acquaintance encountered during Beckett's 1936 travels in Germany, suggested that Beckett might translate poems by Joachim Ringelnatz, pseudonym of Hans Bötticher (1883–1934). Seaman, windowdresser, librarian, minesweeper captain, and postwar cabaret comedian, Ringelnatz the poet did not attract Beckett. Dismissing him as a Rhyme Coolie, Beckett then articulated a virtual credo (which he now dismisses as 'German bilge'). By correcting a very few (mainly typographical) errors of Beckett's typescript, Martin Esslin has rendered the whole letter intelligible, and his translation follows:

Dear Axel Kaun,
Many thanks for your letter. I was on the point of writing to you when it arrived. Then I had to go on my travels, like Ringelnatz's male postage stamp, albeit under less passionate circumstances.

It would be best if I told you immediately and without beating about the bush that Ringelnatz, in my opinion, isn't worth the effort. You will surely not be more disappointed to hear this from me than I am to state it.

I have read through the 3 volumes, have selected 23 poems and have translated 2 of these as samples. The little they have of necessity lost in the process can naturally only be evaluated in relation to what they had to lose, and I must say that I have found this coefficient of loss of quality very small, even in those places where he is most a poet and least a rhyme coolie. It does not follow from this that a translated Ringelnatz could find neither interest nor success with the English public. But in this respect I am totally incapable of arriving at a judgement, as the reactions of the small as well as the large public are becoming more and more enigmatic to me, and, what is worse, of less significance. For I cannot free myself from the naive alternative, at least where literature is concerned, that a matter must either be worthwhile or not worthwhile. And if we have to earn money at any price, let's do it elsewhere.

I have no doubt that as a human being Ringelnatz was of quite extraordinary interest. But as a poet he seems to have shared Goethe's opinion: it is better to write NOTHING than not write at all. But even the Grand Ducal Councillor would have allowed the translator to feel himself unworthy of this high Kakoethes. I should be happy to explain to you my disgust with Ringelnatz's rhyming fury in greater detail, if you feel inclined to understand him. But for the time being I'll spare you. Perhaps you like funeral orations as little as I do.

I could also perhaps advise you of the poems I've selected and send you the sample translations.

— — — — — — — — — — — — — — — — — — — —

I am always glad to receive a letter from you. So please write as frequently and fully as possible. Do you insist that I should do likewise in English? Are you are bored by reading my Geman letters as I am in writing one in English? I should be sorry if you felt that there might be something like a contract between us that I fail to fulfill. An answer is requested.

It is indeed becoming more and more difficult, even senseless, for me to write an official English. And more and more my own language appears to me like a veil that must be torn apart in order to get at the things (or the Nothingness) behind it. Grammar and Style. To me they seem to have become as irrelevant as a Victorian bathing suit or the imperturbability of a true gentleman. A mask. Let us hope the time will come, thank God that in certain circles it has already come, when language is most efficiently used where it is being most efficiently misused. As we cannot eliminate language all at once, we should at least leave nothing undone that might contribute to its falling into disrepute. To bore one hole after another in it, until what lurks behind it — be it something or nothing — begins to seep through; I cannot imagine a higher goal for a writer today. Or is literature alone to remain behind in the old lazy ways that have been so long ago abandoned by music and painting? Is there something paralysingly holy in the vicious nature of the word that is not found in the elements of the other arts? Is there any reason why that terrible materiality of the word surface should not be capable of being dissolved, like for example the sound surface, torn by enormous pauses, of Beethoven's seventh Symphony, so that through whole pages we can perceive nothing but a path of sounds suspended in giddy heights, linking unfathomable abysses of silence? An answer is requested. I know there are people, sensitive and intelligent people, for whom there is no lack of silence. I cannot but assume that they are hard of hearing. For in the forest of symbols, which aren't any, the little birds of interpretation, which isn't any, are never silent.

Of course, for the time being we must be satisfied with little. At first it can only be a matter of somehow finding a method by which we can represent this mocking attitude towards the word, through words. In this dissonance between the means and their use it will perhaps become possible to feel a whisper of that final music or that silence that underlies All.

With such a program, in my opinion, the latest work of Joyce has nothing whatever to do. There it seems rather to be a matter of an apotheosis of the word. Unless perhaps Ascension to Heaven and Descent to Hell are somehow one and the same. How beautiful it would be to be able to believe that that indeed was the case. But for the time being we want to confine ourselves to the mere intention.

Perhaps the logographs of Gertrude Stein are nearer to what I have in mind. At least the texture of language has become porous, if only, alas, quite by chance, and as a consequence of a technique similar to that of Feininger. The unfortunate lady (is she still alive?) is doubtlessly still in love with her vehicle, albeit only in the way in which a mathematician is in love with his figures; a mathematician for whom the solution of the problem is of entirely secondary interest, indeed to whom must the death of his figures appear quite dreadful. To bring this method into relation with that of Joyce, as is the fashion, strikes me as senseless as the attempt, of which I know nothing as yet, to compare Nominalism (in the sense of the Scholastics) with Realism. On the way to this literature of the unword, which is so desirable to me, some form of Nominalist irony might be a necessary stage. But it is not enough for the game to lose some of its sacred seriousness. It should stop. Let us therefore act like that mad (?) mathematician who used a different principle of measurement at each step of his calculation. An assault against words in the name of beauty. In the meantime I am doing nothing at all. Only from time to time I have the consolation, as now, of sinning willy-nilly against a foreign language, as I should love to do with full knowledge and intent against my own — and as I shall do — Deo juvante.

With cordial greetings

Should I return the Ringelnatz volume to you?
Is there an English translation of Trakl?

Les Deux Besoins. Written in 1938, this unpublished essay is found in typescript in the Baker Memorial Library of Dartmouth College. More tersely (and correctly) phrased than the German letter of the previous year, it continues Beckett's research into the imperatives of art, even while it mocks such research. A zoological image from Flaubert, a geometrical diagram, a pre-Socratic anecdote, and parallel scorn for science and theology — these disjunctive paragraphs succeed one another in Beckett's plea for an irrational, interrogative art.

Part II

A. *Other Writers.*

Pieces written for publication in specific periodicals, this occasional criticism displays Beckett's unusual range of mastery — music, painting, French, German, Italian, and Irish literature. Spanning the decade in which he shifted domicile and language, the diversity of material sports a unity of (arrogant) tone, whose limpidity contrasts with the earlier esthetic explorations. These pieces defend the artist against reductive rational criticism.

Schwabenstreich. Spectator March 23, 1934.
Proust in Pieces. Spectator June 23, 1934.
J. B. Leishmann's translation of Rilke's *Poems. Criterion* July, 1934.
Humanistic Quietism. Dublin Magazine July–September, 1934.
Recent Irish Poetry. The Bookman August, 1934 (under the Pseudonym Andrew Belis).
Ex Cathezra, Papini's Dante, The Essential and the Incidental. The Bookman Christmas, 1934.
Censorship in the Saorstat. Commissioned by *The Bookman*, this essay was written in 1935. After *The Bookman* ceased publication, Beckett sent it to his Paris agent George Reavey for *transition*, but it remained unpubished. The typescript is in the Baker Memorial Library of Dartmouth College. Ireland lurks behind the titular Saorstat, derived from Old Testament Saor or Zoar, an iniquitous region redolent of drunkenness and sexual indulgence.
An Imaginative Work. Dublin Magazine July–September, 1936.
Intercessions by Denis Devlin. transition April–May, 1938.
Intercessions by Denis Devlin. transition April–May, 1938. Contemporary with *Les Deux Besoins*, this review also phrases artistic compulsion as 'need'.
MacGreevy on Yeats. Irish Times August 4, 1945.

Part II B. *Self*

Unlike self-conscious pieces intended for publication, Beckett's letters on aspects of his work are unguarded. For sundry reasons, a few of these letters have reached print and are here reprinted, with his permission.

The Possessed. Published anonymously in *T.C.D.* (the Trinity College, Dublin, weekly) on March 12, 1931, this verbal romp is Beckett's rebuttal to an unfavorable review of a performance of *Le Kid*, a parody of Corneille's *Le Cid*, written by Beckett and the French exchange student, Georges Pelorson. *Le Kid* appears to be lost, but Beckett's parody of a drama reviewer proves that clichés live on.

On *Murphy*. This excerpt from a letter to his old friend Thomas McGreevy, July 17, 1936, is quoted in *Samuel Beckett* by Deirdre Bair: New York, Harcourt Brace Jovanovich, 1978.

On Murphy. This excerpt from a letter to his agent George Reavey, November 13, 1936, is quoted in *Samuel Beckett* by Bair.

On works to 1951. This letter to Jérôme Lindon, his French publisher, was first published in English translation in *Beckett at 60*: London, Calder and Boyars, 1967. Original French version appeared in *Beckett*, eds. Bishop and Federman: Paris, L'Herne, 1976.

On *Endgame*. These excerpts from letters to Alan Schneider, Beckett's American director, were first published in *Village Voice*, March 19, 1958.

On *Play*. This letter to the late George Devine (1910–66) was published in *Samuel Beckett: an exhibition*, by James Knowlson: London, Turret Books, 1971. Devine founded London's English Stage Company and directed several Beckett plays at the Royal Court Theatre. 'Jocelyn' is Jocelyn Herbert, designer, who designed the sets.

On *Murphy*. Sighle Kennedy wrote Beckett in connection with her dissertation on *Murphy*, subsequently published as *Murphy's Bed* (Lewisburg: Bucknell University Press, 1971), where this letter appears.

On *Endgame*. These questions and answers appeared in the program of Beckett's 1967 production of *Endgame* (in German) in West Berlin's Schiller Theater Werkstatt.

Part III

Geer van Velde. This paragraph was written for a 1938 exhibition of the Dutch painter's work at the London Gallery of Peggy Guggenheim.

La Peinture des van Velde ou le monde et le pantalon. Written shortly after the end of World War II and Beckett's return from Dublin to France, this essay was commissioned by *Cahiers d'art* in connection with separate exhibitions of the work of the Dutch brothers. It is Beckett's first publication in French, and it points forward to his French creative work: the subtitle and epigraph refer to the joke of Nagg in *Endgame*; 'le tu est la lumière du dit, et toute présence absence' permeates his *Trilogy*. Like Mercier and Camier, who were conceived a year later, the two painter brothers walk toward the same horizon. Like Molloy, Beckett on Bram van Velde finds that words cancel each other. And one is again reminded of Molloy by Beckett's description of Geer's painting:

'Ici tout bouge, nage, fuit, revient, se défait, se refait. Tout cesse, sans cesse.' — a description dismissed as 'literature'. And 'verbal assassination' is Beckett's verdict on his account of these similar, divergent painters.

Peintres de l'empêchement. Sharper and terser than its predecessor, this essay on the van Velde brothers was commissioned by *Derrière le Miroir*, publication of Galerie Maeght in Paris, where it appeared in June, 1948.

Three Dialogues. The best known of Beckett's writings on painting was published in *transition* December, 1949, and it was subsequently translated into French by its author. In whole and in part, in the original English and in French translation, it has been widely quoted.

Henri Hayden, homme-peintre. Written in January, 1952, for a private showing of Hayden's paintings, this piece was published in *Cahiers d'art* of November 1955. Although no other painter is mentioned in the piece, Beckett 'reads' Hayden's landscapes and still lives as impersonal, tragicomic notes on the subject-object crisis, rather than on the new ground of Bram van Velde.

Hayden. This brief anonymous note was written in June, 1960 for a Hayden exhibition at Galerie Suillerot in Paris.

Hommage à Jack B. Yeats. Published in *Les Lettres Nouvelles* (April, 1954), this tribute was written for a Paris exhibition of the eighty-three year old Irish painter. The extraordinary translation was published in a catalogue of Yeats' paintings edited by James White.

Bram van Velde. This paragraph is the introductory epigraph to the deluxe edition of *Bram van Velde* published by *Pozzo* Brothers in Turin, 1961.

Pour Avigdor Arikha. Written in 1966 for a Paris exhibition of Arikha's drawings, this lyric of criticism was translated by Beckett in 1967 for Arikha exhibitions in England and the United States.

Part IV

Human Wishes. Although Beckett filled three notebooks with material for a play on the relationship of Dr Samuel Johnson and Mrs Thrale, only this scenic fragment of 1937 was actually composed. Pauses, repetitions, and formal patterns are strikingly prophetic of his drama to come. This scene was first published in Ruby Cohn's *Just Play*: Princeton, Princeton University Press, 1980.